JOHN SKELTON

by

NAN COOKE CARPENTER

"John Skelton, Tudor poet and laureate, is today enjoying a well-deserved Renaissance. This book . . . is both part of that Renaissance and an explanation of it." From the Preface.

Divided into three sections, *John Skelton* opens with an account of the life of the poet. As university laureate (Cambridge, Oxford, perhaps Louvain, court poet for Henry VII, tutor to one or both of Henry's sons, rector of Diss in Norfolk, and finally royal orator to Henry VIII, Skelton is followed in all the colorful details of his career.

The second and largest section of the book deals with Skelton's works. Treated here are the writings from his Westminster years as court poet to Henry VII, the products of his Diss period — *Philip Sparrow* and *Ware the Hawk* — and finally the rich production of his last years in Westminster as royal orator to Henry VIII. Special attention is paid to the early short lyrics, generally passed over by critics, and to the musical imagery everywhere abundant. Throughout these discussions, Professor Carpenter traces the changing style of the poet from conventional techniques to the final evolution of a unique style of his own — the Skeltonic.

Skelton is viewed, in conclusion, as poet, humanist, and musician, a figure between the Middle Ages and the Renaissance, with characteristics of both. Last of all, his reputation is delineated over the centuries.

Twayne's English Authors Series

Sylvia E. Bowman, Editor

INDIANA UNIVERSITY

John Skelton

 61

By Nan Cooke Carpenter:

Rabelais and Music (Chapel Hill, 1954)

Music in the Medieval and Renaissance Universities (Norman, 1958)

John Skelton

By NAN COOKE CARPENTER

University of Georgia

Twayne Publishers, Inc.   ::   New York

MANUFACTURED IN THE UNITED STATES OF AMERICA

Preface

John Skelton, early Tudor poet and laureate, is today enjoying a well-deserved renaissance. This book, designed for any reader interested in Skelton, is both a part of that renaissance and an explanation for it. The neophyte will find here, one hopes, a pleasant introduction to the poet and a wide enough sampling of his works to feel the perennial charm of his poetry. To the more advanced student, this book offers an account of the poet's life brought up to date in the light of recent scholarship; a critical survey of his work in considerable depth, illuminated by a number of new insights, especially musical ones; and, finally, an evaluation of the laureate as humanist, poet, and musician. This study of Skelton makes plain, too, the need for further investigation in certain areas. For example, the interesting relationship between Skelton and the Scottish poets, William Dunbar especially, has never been thoroughly investigated; and still unsolved are many problems connected with Skelton's whereabouts during the last years of his life.

In the critical analysis of the laureate's works constituting the largest part of this book, I have devoted special care to the short lyrics and other poems that have up to now received little or no attention on the part of critics. I have placed special emphasis, too, upon the poet's musical background and understanding, constantly reflected in his verse—a most important facet of his work almost untouched by all previous commentators. Also, I have pursued the Skelton-Wolsey controversy as deeply as possible through contemporary documents, and have come up with some new conclusions about that relationship.

In entombing the laureate here, I have tried to maintain a proper balance between the readable and the scholarly (and to make the notes as interesting as the text). Except when quoting from older editions, then, I have followed the usual trend among

JOHN SKELTON

Chronology

c. 1460 John Skelton born, probably in Yorkshire.

1478/9 Skelton probably takes a Cambridge degree (Peter-house?).

1483 *Elegy on Edward IV* written.

c. 1485 Translations of *Diodorus Siculus* and of Cicero's *Familiar Letters.*

1488 First year, seemingly, of Skelton's private calendar. Possible laureation (by the King?) at Oxford. Skelton enters service of Henry VII.

1489 By now, Skelton has been laureated by Oxford. (Lost) poem on Prince Arthur's Creation (Arthur, 1486–1502, created Knight of Bath, Prince of Wales, Earl of Chester). First court production: elegy on the Earl of Northumberland. (Lost) poem against Robert Gaguin of the French Embassy.

1490 Skelton praised by Caxton in the *Eneydos* (June 22).

1491 *Mistress Anne* lyrics and other short poems probably written during these early years at court.

1492 Skelton goes to France with King Henry and the court(?). Probable laureation at Louvain.

1493 Skelton laureated by Cambridge University.

1494 Skelton now tutor to Prince Henry (b. 1491). Latin verses to the young Duke of York (Henry created Duke of York).

1495 Skelton entertained in London by Cambridge officials.

1495/6 *Against a Comely Coistrown* composed in Latin and English.

1497 Translation of the *Pélerinage* about this time.

1498 Skelton takes orders: ordained subdeacon, deacon, priest in the same year. Religious lyrics probably written during this year of serious religious study: *Vexilla Regis, Upon a*

Dead Man's Head, Woefully Arrayed. Bouge of Court, first description of court life, composed.

1499 Skelton praised by Erasmus (who comes to England this year) in a *Carmen extemporale. Bouge of Court* printed by Wynken de Worde, Caxton's successor.

1501 Skelton entertained (January-March) by Cambridge officials. May 14: Case of Peter Ottey *vs.* John Skelton. *Speculum principis* written (August) for royal pupil, now in his teens.

1502 April: Payment of forty shillings to the "duc of Yorks scolemaster."

1503 W. Skelton in Westminster (= John?).

1504 April 10: Skelton witnesses a will (first appearance of his name in Diss records). (Lost) *Necromancer* printed by Wynken de Worde ?

1505 Lady Margaret visits Cambridge; Skelton probably made M.A. on this occasion; Cambridge grants him "the same status that he has at Oxford" and the right to wear his royal robe.

1506 Skelton probably in Cambridge: mock elegies (on Adam Uddersall and John Clarke) copied by Vicar of Trumpington. Skelton composes *Lament* for city of Norwich, recently burned.

1508 *Philip Sparrow, Ware the Hawk.*

1509 *The Rose Both White and Red:* Skelton's coronation ode ? A *Palinodium* also addressed to Henry VIII (coronation, June 24). October 21: Skelton on King's pardon roll. December 3: Skelton in Pykerell case at Diss. *Philip Sparrow* denigrated in Barclay's *Ship of Fools.*

1511 Skelton presents his *Speculum principis* (slightly rewritten) and a *Complaint* to the King (at New Year's?). July: Skelton dines with Prior of Westminster. November: Skelton appointed arbiter in ecclesiastical case at Norwich.

1512 Skelton is back at court. *Chronique de Rains* presented to King (another New Year's gift?). Latin epitaphs for tomb in new Lady Chapel in Westminster Abbey. Latin *Eulogy for his Own Times. Calliope* (?).

1513 Skelton probably accompanies King Henry to France. August 28: *Chorus de Dis contra Gallos.* (Battle of Flodden Field against the Scots fought September 9). *Ballade of the Scottyshe King:* first English ballad to be printed (Fawkes). September 22: *Chorus de Dis contra Scottos.* Invective *Against the Scots; Against Dundas.*

1514 *Poems against Garnesche,* the first English flyting (mid-August).

1516 Latin *Elegy on the Countess of Derby.* First poem directed at Wolsey: *Against Venomous Tongues. Magnificence,* only surviving drama.

1518 Skelton probably living in Westminster: his tenement mentioned in Westminster document. *Epitaph on Bedell.*

1519 Skelton praised in Whittington's *Eulogy,* printed by Wynken de Worde.

1520 Skelton's (lost) poem against Lyly (who had composed an epigram against Skelton).

1521 *Speak, Parrot* written late in year while Skelton was with the Howards (probably in Yorkshire). Skelton tutor to young Henry Howard ?

1522 *Elinor Rumming ? Colin Clout.*

1523 *Why Come Ye Not to Court?* final satire against Wolsey. October: *Garland of Laurel* (written in Yorkshire during past several years) published by Fawkes.

1523/4 *The Duke of Albany.*

1525 Tale vi, *Merie Tales of Skelton,* published in Rastell's *Hundred Merry Tales.*

c. 1526 Pynson(?) prints *Dyuers Balettys and Dyties solacyous* (5 short lyrics); *Agaynste a Comely Coystrowne.*

1528 Last published work: *A Replication* (against Cambridge students Thomas Arthur and Thomas Bilney, who abjured their heresy December 8, 1527), with *Envoy* to Wolsey mentioning a promised benefice. May 4: Skelton is witness in a heresy trial.

1529 June 21: Skelton dies in Westminster; payments for candles and peals at his death. Burial in parish Church of St. Margaret.

CHAPTER 1

Life: c. 1460–1529

In parochia de Dis
Non erat sibi similis.

I *Laureate and Court Poet*

WHAT is known of John Skelton's life is based largely upon
two sources: the existing records about him and what he
himself says. Although there are no records relating to his birth
or baptism, so far as is known, it is now generally agreed that the
poet, clergyman, royal tutor, and *orator regius* was born in or
about 1460 in the north of England and most probably in Yorkshire.[1] Little is known of his early life, but it is abundantly clear
that he received somewhere a proper secondary education, possibly as a choirboy, for his knowledge of music is everywhere
paramount in his works. In one poem, he speaks with great affec-
tion of Cambridge, his *alma parens* with whom he claimed son-
ship—"Namque tibi quandam carus alumnus eram"—adding in
a marginal note that Cambridge had first nourished Skelton
laureate with her pap of knowledge.[2] No Skelton listed in Cambridge records during the last decades of the century, however,
has been definitely identified as the poet. One likely candidate
for this honor is a Peterhouse man who proceeded bachelor of
arts, 1478/9; another is a Dominus Skelton, *questionist* (that is,
about to proceed bachelor of arts), on March 18, 1480.[3]

The Other Place also claimed Skelton. By 1490, the printer
William Caxton could speak of him—in the preface to the *Eneydos*—as "late created poete laureate in the vnyuersite of oxen-
forde." [4] A few years later, Skelton was similarly honored with
the only laureateship ever awarded at Cambridge (1493), where
his grace specifically mentions his having been laureated at Oxford and overseas.[5] Popular legends, too, relate the poet to Oxford. In the *Merie Tales of Skelton* (first published in 1567), the
poet is several times associated with this university.

Tale i ("How Skelton came late home to Oxford from Abington") begins, "Skelton was an Englysheman borne as Skogyn was, and hee was educated & broughte vp in Oxfoorde: and there was he made a poete lauriat. And on a tyme he had ben at Abbington to make mery, wher that he had eate salte meates, and hee did com late home to Oxforde, and he did lye in an ine named ye Tabere whyche is now the Angel. . . ." [6] Tale iii is even more definite in assigning Skelton to Oxford: "When Skelton did cum to London, ther were manye men at the table at diner. Amongest all other there was one sayde to Skelton, Be you of Oxforde or of Cambridge a scholer? Skelton sayd, I am of Oxford." [7]

Oxford registers for the years near the end of the century are missing, and so we have no record of Skelton's laureation, which actually amounted to a degree in rhetoric.[8] But the date of this important event may have been 1488, for several reasons. Not only did Caxton speak of Skelton in 1490 as "late created poet laureate," but the poet himself used this title in an elegy written in 1489 (the year of Northumberland's death)—his poem upon the "dolorous death" of the Earl of Northumberland. More interesting than this is the fact that something of great importance happened to him in October or November of the year 1488— something so momentous that he began a private calendar at that time, dating its beginning from the autumn of 1488.[9] In his poems against Garnesche, Skelton speaks proudly of his Oxford laureation in connection with a robe given him by the King:

> A kyng to me myn habyte gaue:
> At Oxforth, the vniversyte,
> Auaunsid I was to that degre;
> By hole consent of theyr senate,
> I was made poet lawreate.[10]

Skelton's Oxford laureation, then, may have inspired him to begin his own personal calendar, of which 1488 was the first year. But it is now fairly certain that another event took place in 1488, even more significant than the laureling and perhaps following closely upon it—Skelton's entrance upon duties at court in the service of King Henry. As court poet, Skelton had his own "habit," a robe of the Tudor colors, white and green, with Calliope embroidered in gold upon it. In a short poem, in both

Latin and English, the laureate answers a question that must
have been put to him more than once: "Why were ye *Calliope*
embrawdred with letters of golde?" Skelton Laureate, he says,
"maketh this aunswere":

> Calliope,
> As ye may se,
> Regent is she
>   Of poetes al,
> Whiche gaue to me
> The high degre
> Laureat to be
>   Of fame royall;
> Whose name enrolde
> With silke and golde
> I dare be bolde
>   Thus for to were. . . .[11]

Although documents relating to his appointment have long
since disappeared, the month of November, 1488, now stands as
the time Skelton first embarked upon royal duties that apparently consisted of celebrating in Latin or English verse for pos-
terity anything of moment done by the King. Skelton's chief
obligation, in other words, was to bring glory upon the court
through the powers of eloquence. The laureate was by no means
the only rhetorician and humanist at court: Henry VII kept many
distinguished foreigners in his service.[12] But Skelton was one of
the very few native Englishmen among the poets and scholars
surrounding the King.

The first poem of which we have knowledge written as part
of Skelton's court duties honored the Earl of Northumberland,
who was killed April 28, 1489, by the people of his own shire
(the Earl was Lord Lieutenant for Yorkshire at the time) while
trying to raise taxes (of which he himself highly disapproved)
by order of the King.[13] Before becoming court poet, however,
Skelton had perhaps written an elegy for Edward IV, who died
in 1483. And according to Caxton, in the preface to the *Eneydos,*
Skelton had already become distinguished as a translator, having
"late translated the epystlys of Tulle / and the boke of dyodorus
syculus, and diuerse other werkes oute of latyn in-to englysshe,
not in rude and olde langage, but in polysshed and ornate termes

craftely" [14]—that is, Cicero's *Familiar Letters* and the world history of Diodorus Siculus. In the lengthy poem written near the end of his life, the *Garland of Laurel,* Skelton himself tells of having made "Of Tullis Familiars the translacyoun"; and he lists among his works, "Diodorus Siculus of my translacyon / Out of fresshe Latine into owre Englysshe playne." [15] The translation of Cicero has not survived; that of Diodorus has recently become available to us.

Several "lost" poems mentioned by Skelton in his *Garland of Laurel* also obviously date from the year 1489. One of these is *Prince Arturis Creacyoun,* possibly a (Latin?) poem in honor of Arthur's becoming Prince of Wales and Earl of Chester on October 1, 1489. "The Recule ageinst Gaguyne of the Frenshe nacyoun" also appears in Skelton's catalogue of his own works. This refers to Robert Gaguin, distinguished French humanist and leader of an embassy to England to treat of the marriage of Charles VIII of France and Anne of Brittany, in August and September, 1489.[16] The embassy was unsuccessful, and Gaguin showed his displeasure by aiming a poetical diatribe against Henry. But the King's poets came to his rescue with a flourish; John Skelton supported his monarch, along with the Italians Gigli, Carmeliano, and Vitelli. Bernard André, blind poet and teacher of French to Prince Arthur, has left an account of the affair, which he sums up happily: the French ambassador, "hooted and hissed out by these . . . compositions . . . departed in a great rage." Neither Skelton's poem honoring Prince Arthur nor his *recule* dishonoring Gaguin has survived.

Meantime, the court poet continued to receive new honors. Early in the 1490's, he was awarded the laurel by the University of Louvain; and it seems likely that politics had something to do with the laureation. His Cambridge grace, we recall, speaks of his having been made poet laureate *in partibus transmarinis*— across the seas, somewhere. A contemporary—the grammarian and Oxford laureate, Robert Whittington—informs us that the university honoring the poet was Louvain, for Whittington addressed to Skelton a long eulogy: "In Clarissimi Scheltonis *Louaniensis* Poetae Laudes Epigramma." [17] Interestingly enough, this university had a long history of emphasis upon poetry and rhetoric, with an endowed chair in that discipline, held in 1492 by

Francesco de Crema.[18] It seems quite likely that Skelton received his award in this year, and he may have been present for the ceremony.

For a brief period in 1492 Maximilian, King of the Romans, was allied with Henry of England against Charles VIII of France. But all this changed on November 3, 1492, with the Treaty of Etaples, when Henry withdrew his support for Maximilian. One of Skelton's latest biographers suggests that Skelton accompanied King Henry on his sortie into France in 1492, and that the poet could easily have ridden from Calais to visit the Flemish university and the newly arrived professor of rhetoric, Francesco.[19] The University of Louvain may well have honored the Oxford laureate as a graceful compliment to the King. Skelton's own *alma mater*, as we have seen, was not slow in bestowing a similar honor upon her now distinguished son. His grace for the only laureling known to have taken place at Cambridge (1493) definitely stated that the poet "crowned with laurel at Oxford and overseas, be decorated by us with the same." [20]

II *Royal Tutor*

A few years after Skelton's debut in London, he assumed some additional duties that had an important effect upon the later course of his life. He became tutor to the future King of England, Prince Henry, who as a child was destined for a career in the Church.[21] Skelton's obvious adherence to the old ways of learning may have recommended him strongly to Henry VII. But the prince's education was largely in the small, fine hands of his grandmother—the Lady Margaret, Countess of Richmond and a great power at court; and she may have been guided in the choice of a schoolmaster for the prince by her spiritual advisor, John Fisher, Master of Grammar, Cambridge, 1480, and therefore at Cambridge at the same time as Skelton—if our poet was indeed there in the late 1470's.[22] Born in 1491, Prince Henry was created Duke of York in 1494 at a splendid ceremony held in Westminster Abbey. The court poet quite properly celebrated this event with some Latin verses, "*Carmen ad principem, quando insignitus erat ducis Ebor. titulo.*" [23] Some years later in his poems against Garnesche, Skelton proudly speaks of his duties as tutor to the prince:

> The honor of Englond I lernyd to spelle,
> In dygnyte roialle that doth excelle:
> Note and marke wyl thys parcele;
> I yaue hym drynke of the sugryd welle
> Of Eliconys waters crystallyne,
> Aqueintyng hym with the Musys nyne.[24]

A few lines later in the same poem, Skelton implies that he was the prince's first tutor: "It plesyth that noble prince roialle / Me as hys master for to calle / In hys lernyng primordialle."

Although many opinions have been expressed, no one knows for certain whether Skelton had two little princes in his charge or only one. An early biographer of the poet, John Bale, simply calls him "royal preceptor."[25] Skelton's *Speculum principis* is addressed, at its learned editor points out, to "princes," which, of course, may be pure formality; for its author addresses himself to all young rulers.[26] Moreover, Caxton's *Eneydos*, which extols Skelton in the preface, is dedicated to Prince Arthur. What better scholar to defer to, suggests Professor Salter, than the boy's official tutor, who is asked "to expowne and englysshe euery diffyculte that is therein."[27] Skelton's latest biographers are inclined to think that the laureate was tutor to Prince Henry alone. One might point out that in the verses cited above, the poet himself speaks of "the honor of England" and of giving "him" drink from Helicon's well and acquainting "him" with the Muses. On the other hand, in a poem written many years after Arthur's death when Henry had long since been established as King, there is little reason for bringing in the older lad, even if the poet had been his preceptor.

It is interesting to speculate upon Skelton's other duties at court during his years in the service of Henry VII. He was undoubtedly an active participant in the production of court entertainments, although only one of his own dramas survives. Indeed, his famous poem expressing the idea of the so-called Tudor myth—"The Rose Both White and Red"—owes its survival to the fact that an autograph copy was preserved between the leaves of an account book of the royal revels. Several of Skelton's poems written during this period of his life ("Mannerly Margery," "Jolly Rutterkin") were set to music by no less a musician than William Cornish—royal impresario, music master of the children of Westminster Abbey, and later (1509) Master of the

Children of the Chapel Royal. Significantly, too, the only manuscript copy of Skelton's *Diodorus Siculus* in existence was written
out for Robert Pen—like Cornish, a Gentleman of the Chapel
Royal—another link connecting Skelton with the King's Chapel.[28]
It is pleasant to imagine the poet and scholar encouraging his
small charge in musical studies. For music was an art which
Caxton had praised in Skelton ("And also he hath redde the ix.
muses, and vnderstande theyr musicalle scyences") and one in
which Henry became more than proficient.[29]

Meanwhile, Skelton kept up his academic connections. We
have records of his dining with Cambridge men who had come
up to London to help clear up a university lawsuit.[30] These men
on university business in 1495 kept a meticulous expense account,
one item of which includes "master Skelton's" meal on the official
list of expenses "because he was with the Bishop of Salisbury."
The latter was John Blythe, not only Bishop of Salisbury but also
Chancellor of the University—and the fact that the poet was in
such distinguished company assured his being wined and dined
at university expense. A few days later, he was taken to lunch
at Symson's in Fleet Street by another member of the group,
John Suckling (Syclyng), Master of Godshouse (later, Christ's
College). One hopes that the poet laureate was able to assist his
alma mater in getting the business successfully concluded in
London.

Among the "lost" works mentioned in the *Garland of Laurel* are
some that were evidently of a moral nature—probably composed
during the years when Skelton was tutor to Prince Henry. We are
told, for instance, that the poet translated a long French poem for
the Lady Margaret, the Countess of Richmond:

> Of my ladys grace at the contemplacyoun,
> Owt of Frenshe into Englysshe prose,
> Of Mannes Lyfe the Peregrynacioun,
> He did translate, enterprete, and disclose.[31]

This refers to the moral allegory, *La Pélerinage de la vie hu-
maine*, by Guillaume de Guilleville, of which Caxton and Pynson
printed translations, and the poet John Lydgate made a translation. Some of the other lost items in Skelton's list may also have
been undertaken at the Countess's request; for example, Skelton
tells that he had written "Also a devoute Prayer to Moyses

hornis, / Metrifyde merely, medelyd with scornis."[32] The poet's
marginal note ("Exaltabuntur cornus justi: Psalmo.") as well as
the description "devout prayer" gives us some hint as to the obviously devotional nature of the work. The *Pélerinage* and perhaps other moral poems produced for the King's mother relate
Skelton inevitably to a record from December, 1497, that is especially interesting: payment of sixty-six shillings and eightpence
(three pounds, six and eight—a goodly sum indeed!) "to my
lady the kinges moder poete."[33]

No doubt this small but vigorous lady was responsible for her
poet's taking orders while he was at court. By now he was an
Oxford Master of Arts, and he may also have had a degree in
theology.[34] During 1498, he became a full-fledged priest of the
Church; for, once decided upon, this course of events went
through in a hurry, as Skelton was ordained respectively subdeacon, deacon, and priest by the Bishop of London, in March,
April, and June.[35] (Interestingly enough, the famous "boy bachelor" of Oxford, young Thomas Wolsey, also entered the priesthood in March, 1498.[36]) A group of religious poems—*Vexilla
Regis, Upon a Dead Man's Head,* and *Woefully Arrayed*—may
have been inspired by the laureate's studies and reflections when
he was consecrated priest. As Peter Green observes in his excellent little monograph on Skelton, the poet may have been stirred
at the time of his consecration to an active poetic assertion of
faith never again quite recaptured.[37] King Henry himself at-
tended what may have been the new priest's first mass, celebrated a few months after his ordination (November 16, 1498),
and gave the new clergyman a generous gift in honor of the
occasion.[38] This royal gift of twenty shillings was about three
times the King's usual Sunday offering.

Skelton's first major poem, the *Bouge of Court,* a dream allegory about the evils of court life, was written soon after he entered upon the life of a priest; and it marks a turning-away from
the old life at court of which he had seen so much. As royal poet,
he himself was entitled to "bouge of court"—free board and
lodging. As the prince's tutor, he lived with his young charge at
Prince Henry's home—maintained quite apart from that of his
brother Arthur—at Eltham, near Greenwich. In this lovely rural
setting—the stately manor of which is still standing—Skelton
and the embryonic Archbishop of Canterbury studied and per-

haps made music together. With several servants, a good salary, fairly light duties, and freedom to join his friends at nearby Greenwich, Sheen, or Westminster, the poet must have enjoyed a pleasant life.[39] At least once during the summer of 1499 Skelton's poetic gifts and diligence with his young pupil were richly appreciated.

For in June of this year, the great Dutch scholar Desiderius Erasmus came to England for the first time, in company with his pupil Lord Mountjoy, at whose home at Greenwich he stayed. We know that on one occasion he was taken to see the children at the Royal Palace by Sir Thomas More, who owned a house at nearby Eltham: Erasmus himself has left an account of this visit in one of his letters.[40] It seems that on this occasion—arranged in advance by More and Skelton? —More brought along a manuscript to present to young Prince Henry, but Erasmus had not been forewarned, and so had no poem to contribute. Even more shattering was a note he received at dinner from Henry, asking for some evidence of his poetical gift. Naturally, the distinguished visitor worked hard the next few days putting together a little volume of verse for his royal acquaintance. In a dedication to the prince, he praises enthusiastically Henry's tutor, whom he would surely have met at Eltham: Erasmus would urge the prince to grow in virtues, he says, "were it not that you are of your own accord already, as they say, under way with all sails set, and have with you Skelton, that incomparable light and ornament of British letters, who can not only kindle your studies, but bring them to a happy conclusion." [41]

The ode composed by Erasmus for a royal gift is the poem *De laudibus Britanniae,* in which are several lines about the prince's tutor: "Now the boy Henry, happy in the name of his father, is introduced to the sacred fountains of the Muses by the poet Skelton." [42] And along with the ode went a *Carmen extemporale* to Skelton himself. This seems, from its opening lines, to have been written in response to a eulogistic poem to the famous visitor written by the British laureate; for it begins, "O Skelton, worthy of eternal fame, / Why should thy fount of speech pour on my name / The meed of praise . . . ?" [43]

Two years after the encounter with Erasmus, other records indicate that Skelton was again wined and dined at the expense of the University of Cambridge. Early in 1501, Master Suckling and other university officials were once more in Westminster on business about a controversy between town and gown. The expense account of this group indicates that on three occasions a day spent on university business was pleasantly terminated by entertaining the royal tutor and Cambridge alumnus to supper —at sixpence each time.[44] On another occasion, the poet sat in Suckling's room, and, as one recent biographer interprets the record, "talked over a penny drink before a penny fire." [45] If the stories current about Skelton (*The Merie Tales of Skelton*) contain even a shred of truth—and they evidently contain much more—these suppers and conversations must have been stimulating as well as relaxing, heightened by the poet's sharp repartee and sparkling wit.

Perhaps it was his sharp tongue that got him into trouble later in the same year (1501). Although the record is difficult to interpret, it seems that Skelton (if it actually was the poet: no other John Skelton is known to have been busy at court at this time) angered one of the royal chaplains, Peter Ottey or Ottley, and was bound under penalty of forty pounds to appear before the Bishop of Ely for trial.[46] Nothing further is known of this case.

It was in 1501, too, that Skelton wrote out—perhaps composing for the first time—his *Speculum principis*, which he signs, "At Eltham, 28 August 1501." [47] The "little mirror" was written, in the words of its author, "for the princes in their minority." Some years later, after Henry had become King, the poet revised the work a bit and presented it formally to his former pupil.

Skelton's duties as preceptor appear to have come to an end in 1502. In April of this year, Prince Arthur died, and the household of the new heir to the throne was drastically reorganized. A record of April 29, 1502, tells us that the "duc of yorks scolemaster" was paid forty shillings by the King.[48] Prince Henry, now in his teens, would of course enter upon an advanced type of instruction in keeping with his new role in the kingdom; and in due course one finds a certain William Hone or Hoone in residence as the future King's tutor.[49] One other notice from 1502 (June 10) states that one John Skelton was committed to prison ("carceribus genitoris domini regis") in a case involving churchmen and court officials.[50] The poet—if this was he—was guilty only of standing surety for an unpaid debt; and the charge,

which appears to have been a mere formality, was in fact
dropped when the loan was repaid.

III   *Rector of Diss*

Skelton's biographers agree that he terminated his official duties at court soon after Prince Arthur's death in 1502; but the
old notion that he was dismissed from court and exiled to Diss
has long since gone out of favor. Actually, no one knows just
when he left Westminster. By 1504, however, John Skelton had
entered upon a new life, for a document from this year (April
10) finds him living in the little Norfolk town of Diss, presiding
over the parish there. The document in question is the will of
one Margery Cowper of Diss, which Skelton witnessed: "Theise
beyng witnesse Master Iohn Skelton laureat parson of disse and
Sir Iohn Clarke sowle preest of the same towne." [51] It seems
fairly certain that the laureate was given the living of the little
market town in prosperous East Anglia by the Lady Margaret—
in whose gift it was—following the general reshuffle at court
after the death of Arthur, and that the comfortable benefice was
perhaps a reward for his years of service at court.

During the next year, Skelton received another academic
honor, this one from the University of Cambridge, situated in
East Anglia within easy riding distance of Diss. In the spring
of that year, the Lady Margaret paid the university a state visit,
during which she concluded arrangements for her splendid new
foundation, Christ's College, expanded from the old Godshouse,
with Suckling as head.[52] The new college officially dates from
May 1, 1505. Skelton's Cambridge grace dates from the same
year. Perhaps it was during this royal visit that the poet's own
alma mater granted him "the same status here that he has at
Oxford and the right to wear the robe granted him by the king." [53]

The distinguished list of graduates at this time indicates that
the awarding of these degrees had some special significance.
William Hoone was also incorporated M.A. from Oxford, and
two musical degrees were awarded: both Humphrey Frevill and
Robert Cowper commenced doctor of music—a somewhat rare
occurrence and one that often guaranteed the performance of
some good music at the commencement exercises.[54] Moreover,
anyone familiar with or baffled by customs with regard to the

wearing of robes today in Oxford or Cambridge can appreciate
the importance of the special dispensation given the King's laureate so that he could wear his royal gown—the one with *Calliope*
embroidered upon it in gold. (Perhaps his little poem *Calliope*
was written to answer those who queried him about his strange-
looking robe as he moved about the lovely "backs" of Cambridge.) It is obvious that Skelton was allowed his unique garb
because he was the university's only laureate and Cambridge had
no fixed regulations about gowns for laureates.[55]

From 1504 for some years, now, Skelton remained at Diss,
going occasionally to London. A change in his career was paral-
leled by a change in poetic style, for his most famous "Skeltonic"
poems were written during his years at Diss: *A Devout Trental
for John Clarke, Philip Sparrow, Ware the Hawk,* and *Elinor
Rumming,* among others. Distinguished with M.A. status and the
proud privilege of wearing his royal robe, and finding Diss only
a day's ride from Cambridge, Skelton must have made more
than one visit to his university. We know that he was in Cambridge in 1507, for two of his poems were copied out on January
5 of that year by the university scribe, the Vicar of Trumpington.[56] These poems were his mock epitaphs on the "two knaves"
of Diss, John Clarke and Adam Uddersall. His *Lamentation* for
the city of Norwich—virtually destroyed by fire—also dates from
1507.

A number of rather racy stories grew up about the Rector of
Diss, who must have been a peculiarly colorful clergyman. These
Merie Tales of Skelton, published for the most part long after
the poet's death, show Skelton to have been, as Peter Green
points out,[57] the kind of person—like Dylan Thomas—around
whom legends tended to accumulate. Although much of the
material in the *Tales* is typical jestbook fare and must be dis-
counted, there must have been at least some fire responsible for
all the Rabelaisian smoke. The author of the stories often shows
familiarity with the Oxford of Skelton's day, and one of the *Tales*
(about Skelton's gift of Alpha and Omega to the Bishop of Norwich) was actually current during the poet's lifetime since it
was included in a collection called *A Hundred Merry Tales,* published by Rastell about 1525.[58]

Reading through the stories, one finds many facts about Skelton that are historically accurate: that he was educated at Ox-

ford, was poet laureate, hated heretics, was a familiar of "the
king's court," Rector of Diss, and an acquaintance of Wolsey, by
whom he was imprisoned and pardoned. Even if much of the
ribald narrative is not true, the tales are of inestimable value in
giving one an insight into the character and personality of this
great eccentric, sharp-tongued clergyman, and witty conversation-
alist. The stories most often cited have to do with his being in
great disfavor with the Bishop of Norwich, largely because he
kept a mistress. ("Skelton dyd keepe a musket at Dys, vpon the
which he was complayned on to the bishop of Norwych," Tale vi
begins.) The famous tale of Alpha and Omega is a merry jest
about how he placated the Bishop with a couple of capons—
Alpha and Omega—one being the first gift ever presented, the
other the last.[59] On another occasion, the priest is shown furiously telling off his congregation, who had complained of him
to the Bishop. To pound home his thesis and emphasize his point
with a genuine *argumentum ad oculos,* he had his illegitimate
child brought in and displayed it naked for all the church to see.
Underlining the fact that the child was well formed and perfect
in all its limbs, the rector argued that he was therefore blame-
less in having begotten the child.[60]

Tale x tells that Cardinal Wolsey asked the poet to write an
epitaph for his very "regall tombe" in Westminster. When Skelton understood the cost of the tomb ("more pertaynyng for an
emperoure or a maxymyous kynge, then for suche a man as he
was"), he said to the prelate, "if it shall like your grace to creepe
into thys tombe whiles you be alyue, I can make an epitaphe;
for I am sure that when you be dead you shall neuer haue
it." This time the poet proved to be a good prophet—"The
whyche was verifyed of truthe," the story concludes; for Wolsey
never was buried in this tomb, or even in Westminster.[61] The
story that Skelton was imprisoned by Wolsey and later released
by him (Tale xiv) is an anecdote that turns on a bit of Skeltonic wit—always eagerly anticipated by his friends, apparently:
"Thassistence desirid that he might haue [a boun] graunted, for
they thought it should be some merye pastime that he wyll
shewe your grace. Say on, thou hore head, sayd the cardynall to
Skelton. I pray your grace to let me lye doune and wallow, for
I can kneele no longer."

Several of the tales are anecdotes about Skelton's sharp and often ribald way of dealing with certain friars. This is, of course, a favorite jestbook topic, but some of Skelton's dealings have gone down as recorded fact. Edward Braynewode, in his early life of the poet printed by John Bale in his great *Index of British Writers*, says that Skelton continually waged war with the friars, especially the Dominicans; and Braynewode also tells about Skelton's offending the Bishop by keeping a mistress whom he secretly married.[62] Certainly the sharp wit, forthrightness of speech and action, and impatience with anything that smacked of hypocrisy associated with Skelton in *The Merie Tales* are all to be found, as we shall see, in much of the verse written by the Rector of Diss.

While Skelton was living at Diss, Henry VII died (April 21, 1509) and was succeeded by the poet's former pupil. Like many others, the laureate probably came up to London to present a gift to the new King at his coronation (June 24, 1509). No record of such a trip exists, but in the nineteenth century there was discovered among the revels accounts in the Treasury Records a poem that seems the perfect answer for such an occasion —"A Lawde and Prayse Made for Our Souereigne Lord the King." [63] Filled with praise for the new monarch and proudly signed "British laureate" ("Per me laurigerum Britonum Skeltonida vatem"), the verses are now universally considered to be Skelton's coronation gift to Henry VIII. (Is this poem "The Boke of the Rosiar" mentioned in the *Garland of Laurel*?)

Beginning with the lines, "The Rose both White and Rede / In one Rose now dothe grow," the poem is one of the earliest literary expressions of the Tudor myth, with its basic image of the union of the two roses representing the families of Lancaster and York.[64] It must have been about this time—and it may also have been for the coronation—that Skelton composed a set of Latin verses, "Ad serenissimam iam nunc suam maiestatem regiam, Skeltonidis Laureati non ignobile palinodium, etc." [65] Like the English poem, this *palinodium* is lavish in praise of the new King, who is compared to Hector, Scipio the Great, Marcellus, and finally Jupiter.

In the autumn of this year (October 21, 1509), Skelton's name was found, with many others, on the King's pardon-roll.[66] This procedure, however, is known to have been a pure formality, a precautionary measure undertaken by anyone who ever had

come or ever might come athwart the law. Two other records
from about this time support one strong characteristic that colors
much of Skelton's verse—his traditional orthodoxy and his great
hatred of the new Lutheran heresy. These records deal with two
cases tried by the episcopal court at Norwich (1509–11). The
first of them (December 3, 1509) has to do with one Thomas
Pykerell (Pickerel), who was cited to appear before the court
to answer inquiries about the health of his soul—*"pro anima sua
salute"*—the complainant being John Skelton, Rector of Diss.[67]
The defendant failed to appear this time and twice again, after
which (February 4, 1510), he was declared "suspensus"—that is,
forbidden to enter the church. The other case (November, 1511)
centers upon Master William Dale, Rector of Redgrave, a town
not far from Diss (whose rector in 1500, incidentally, had been
Thomas Wolsey). Dale was apparently not able to answer all
charges brought against him, and so Bishop Nikke appointed
two arbiters to settle the case, one of them being Master Skelton.[68] Obviously the arbiters were able to settle the matter successfully: for Dale satisfied the Bishop with a letter of correction
and the case never came again to court.

IV *Royal Orator, Westminster*

About this time, and even before the Norwich case was concluded, the Rector of Diss became once again a resident of London. After 1511, his name no longer appears in the Diss registers,
his duties apparently being performed by substitute priests,
whose names do appear in the records.[69] On July 5 of that year
(a fast day), Skelton had been in London dining with the Prior
of Westminster Abbey: "this day at dyner with your maistrchip
the Soffrecan and Skelton the poet with others," reads the marginal note beside the list of expenses for various types of fish
composing this meal.[70] This seems to have been the poet's first
connection with Westminster after his return to London. It was
by no means his last. Actually, he apparently never lived anywhere else—except for long visits to Yorkshire—and in due
course he was buried in the parish church there.

Sometime after Henry's accession, Skelton copied out the
treatise he had earlier written for his royal pupil, his *Speculum
principis*, added a new dedication to it, and presented it to the
King.[71] Bound up along with the little "mirror" was the poem

on Henry's becoming Duke of York and the Latin verses to him on his accession—all a gentle reminder that his former tutor was available for service at court. This collection is not signed *orator regius,* a title Skelton assumed in 1512; and so we may assume that the work was presented to the new King soon after his accession. At the end of the little pedagogical treatise and the Latin eulogies, however, are some lines of quite a different kind, much stronger in tone and most revealing of Skelton's outlook at the time.

This *Complaint* is a remarkable example of the laureate's combination of humor on the one hand and seriousness on the other, of lightness and of near-tragic heaviness, as the poet introduces himself, "Skelton Laureate, onetime royal tutor, quiet in soliloquy with himself, as a man wholly given over to oblivion, or like one dead from the heart." After bemoaning his fate—upon him "neither the king's munificence nor fortune's blessing has so far deigned to smile"—he ends with a few succinct precepts that he drums home like a true schoolmaster: "Grow strong, prince, easily a prince of all princes. Understand that a king must rule and not be ruled. Listen to Samuel, read Daniel, banish Ishmael. Banish! Banish!"

As history proved later, this was good advice to Henry, who was already coming under the influence of his Royal Almoner and Counsellor—Thomas Wolsey.[72] One further gift Skelton presented the King before 1512—a manuscript copy of the old *Chronique de Rains,* about Richard the Lion-Hearted, probably once read by Skelton's young pupil, now annotated and furnished with a new dedication to the King.[73] This, too, was obviously meant to be a potent reminder that the "humble poet Skelton" was eagerly awaiting favor from the monarch (as indeed were many other poets and writers). "Go, my book, in haste," he says: "prostrate yourself before the king and commend me to him, his humble poet Skelton. Above all, recount to his majesty the famous battles waged by England's greatest hero, Richard, first of our race. . . ."

Skelton's persistence finally triumphed. In the spring of 1512 —or perhaps in 1513—he was formally recognized by letters patent as *orator regius,* court poet and rhetorician to Henry VIII.[74] He immediately began using his new title and flaunted it proudly the rest of his life. Just what his position entailed is not altogether clear: an orator seems to have been a combination of poet and secretary. Skelton may have served his King as secretary, and he certainly served him well in several capacities as poet, producing odes of victory, one or more interludes to entertain the court, a "flyting" against an obnoxious courtier, epitaphs for deceased royalty, and lyrics of various kinds.

If Skelton facetiously refused to write an epitaph for Cardinal Wolsey, as the compiler of the *Merie Tales* would have us believe, he graciously undertook to produce some very distinguished ones for royalty itself. In fact, two of these poems constitute the first official production, of which we know, on the part of the newly appointed royal orator. These were written at the request of John Islip, Abbot of Westminster Abbey, in 1512, as Skelton himself tells us in the epitaph for Henry VII ("ad sinceram contemplationem reverendi in Christo patris ac domini, domini Johannis Islippae, Abbatis Westmonasteriensis optime meriti, anno domini MDXII . . ."). This fits with what Braynewode says of Skelton's friendship with Islip—that the poet found favor with him when he sought sanctuary in Westminster in order to escape the wrath of Wolsey.[75] One special interest of Islip at this time was the beautiful new Lady Chapel, then under construction, where the bodies of Henry VII, his Queen, and his mother were to lie forever.

Since Skelton was never one to miss an opportunity to praise his new ruler and old pupil, the first of the epitaphs requested by the Abbot to adorn the tombs in the new chapel (*Eulogium pro suorum temporum conditione*) turned out to be not so much a memorial for Henry VII as a eulogy for his successor—*"Noster honor solus, filius, ecce, suus!"* Nonetheless, it must have pleased the Abbot, for it was duly hung in the Chapel of Henry VII.[76] In the poem to Henry VII, Skelton emphasizes his own new title by setting it first in the superscription preceding the verses: "Orator regius Skeltonis laureatus in singulare meritissimumque præconium nobilissimi principis Henrici septimi. . . ." This epitaph, too, was duly hung in the chapel for all to wonder at.

In 1516, the laureate penned another set of verses to be hung in the chapel—an *Elegia* for the late King's mother, the Lady Margaret Beaufort. More than a century later, John Weever, visiting the Abbey in order to describe its funeral monuments at firsthand, found the poem still hanging there. "Here lieth

buried in one of the stateliest Monuments of Europe . . . ,"
Weever writes, "the body of *Henry* the seuenth. . . . This glori-
ous rich Tombe is compassed about with verses, penned by that
Poet *Laureat* (as he stiles himselfe) and Kings Orator, *Iohn
Skelton*." [77]

The year 1513 was marked by two events of great importance
on the political scene.[78] First of all, at the end of June, Henry
VIII—under the influence, of course, of Wolsey—set out for
Calais for a three-month campaign in France. This resulted in the
Battle of the Spurs and in the easy capture of two towns,
Thérouenne and Tournai. Meanwhile, at home the Battle of Flodden Field (September 9) was all the news—the great English
victory under the Earl of Surrey over the Scots under James IV.
In celebration of both these victories, the King's orator rose nobly
to the occasion. He first produced an ode "super triumphali victoria contra Gallos," which he says the Choir of Diss sang on the
eve of the feast of St. John (August 28): "Chorus de Dis, &c . . .
cantavit solemniter hoc elogium in profesto divi Johannis ad decollationem." [79] A few weeks later (September 22), he sounded
forth in Latin hexameters a *Chorus de Dis contra Scottos*, a great
spasm of rejoicing that King James lies dead. Meantime, he had
rushed to produce his *Ballade of the Scottysshe Kynge* quickly,
without waiting to find out the facts of James's death—whose fate
was unknown at first.[80] And sometime later, he revised and added
to his earlier Ballade, producing a great burst of English invective *Against the Scots*.[81] Here he glories in the victory of September 9, when James did indeed lose his life.

And where was the laureate when he was singing his King's
praises so gloriously? The fact that the two Latin poems refer to
the *Chorus de Dis* has caused considerable disagreement among
Skelton's biographers.[82] It seems more than likely, however, that
he was in France with hundreds of other court people, including
priests, secretaries, musicians, and assorted gentlemen of the
Chapel, for Henry's entourage was magnificent indeed. Among
others who embarked with the King—and the list is so extraordinary that one would like to quote all of it—were "the King's
chapel, 115; the King's secretary of Latin, 5 . . . ; gentlemen
ushers, sewers, grooms, and pages, with Petre de Brecia [Car-
melianus], luter; the King's henxemen; the King's trumpeter; the
King's minstrels and players, 10 . . . ; the King's household." [83]

It would have been quite out of character for the royal orator, who gloried in his title and his robe, to have missed such an opportunity as this. Skelton tells us in the superscription to his Latin paean of victory over the French that this piece was sung on August 28. The historians tell us that the decision to raze the walls of the captured city of Thérouenne was not taken until August 26. And so the poet must have been on hand to have known about it. Skelton's Latin *Chorus* against the Scots, a parody on the old processional hymn of Fortunatus, *Salve, festa die,* was perfectly suited to the great celebration on September 22 when —according to the historian Hall—the Tent of the Cloth of Gold was set up, the Gentlemen of the Chapel sang Mass and the *Te Deum,* and Bishop Fisher preached on the death of James of Scotland.[84] Diss, obviously, represented Skelton himself; and the *Chorus* was the contribution of the Rector of Diss to this great ecclesiastical celebration.

Before the end of the year, Skelton was apparently back in Westminster for good, although officially he was still Rector of Diss. He may have been on hand to welcome home the young King, who returned from France late in September and met his Queen in Richmond. Among Henry's retinue in France was one Christopher Garnesche, Sergeant of the King's Tent and also in charge of revels, whose duty it was, among other things, to see that the cloth-of-gold tent was in good repair.[85] Garnesche was knighted for his services in France, and was also a member of the embassy sent over later by Henry to arrange the marriage of Henry's sister Mary to the aging Louis XII. And finally Garnesche was a partisan of Wolsey, who was very much on the rise and more powerful than ever: in January, 1514, Wolsey became Bishop of Lincoln and, in July, Archbishop of York.[86] Garneshe's friendship with the prelate would alone perhaps make him an adversary of the royal orator. At any rate, this is the man with whom Skelton, probably in August, 1514, engaged in a "flyting," a great duel of invective. It was actually "by the kynges most noble commaundment," as Skelton proudly states at the end of each section of his poem, that this contest in abuse, the first example of flyting in English, was arranged and carried off, undoubtedly to the great amusement of the court.

During the remaining years of his life, the poet continued to be associated with Westminster. His home within the Abbey

precinct is the subject of a document of 1518, when he appears
to have changed landladies.[87] And his satirical epitaph on William
Bedell [88] also relates him to Westminster, although this vitupera-
tive memorial could never have been hung over the dead man's
tomb by Abbot Islip. The poet would have had many opportunities to cross swords with Bedell, who had been steward to
the Lady Margaret—and the Countess, we recall, not only looked
after Henry's education but also held the living at Diss. In spite
of Bedell's promiscuous goings-on "with a wench of evil life"
in Oxford, he was a person of enough standing to ask in his will
to be buried in the new Lady Chapel at Westminster. Skelton's
poem "In Bedel, quondam Belial incarnatum, devotum epita-
phium"—an epitaph on Bedell, sometime Belial incarnate—is a
terrific blast at the pious steward. One wonders how the good
Abbot reacted—if indeed he requested this tribute of the court
poet for one recently buried (1518) in the beautiful new chapel
—when he was handed a poem containing these ribald lines:

> *Mortuus est asinus,*
> *Qui pinxit mulum*
> *Hic jacet barbarus;*
> The deuill kys his *culum! Amen.*

But Skelton's epitaph on Bedell was only the flare-up of a
moment. During these last years in London, the royal orator took
his role seriously and produced his long major poems. The first
of these, *Magnificence,* is his only surviving drama (in the *Garland of Laurel* he mentions several others), written in 1516 for
production at court. This political satire was an interlude glorifying the young King and also warning him against the all-
powerful Wolsey, who had become both cardinal and chancellor
in the same year (1515),[89] and who from now on was to feel
more than once the sharp bite of Skelton's pen. *Against Venomous
Tongues* (1516) is one of the first of these attacks; but the
magnum opus directed against Wolsey is the long and elusive
poem *Speak, Parrot,* written at the time of Wolsey's embassy to
France and Belgium, 1521. For the Cardinal, who represented
to Skelton excesses in Church and government, had set out in
August with a huge entourage ostensibly to arbitrate between
Francis I and Charles V, but actually to hold off Francis as long
as possible before openly siding with Charles.[90] Wolsey returned

in November, having accomplished very little; and the next year England and France were at war.

Speak, Parrot is perhaps the most difficult of all Skelton's poems to interpret, couched as it is in what Spenser would call "continued Allegory or darke conceit." The next poem aimed at Wolsey, *Colin Clout* (1522), is much more straightforward satire. Largely directed at excesses in the Church, the verses are spoken by the innocent Colin, representative of the people. The last great blast against the Cardinal was written not long after— *Why Come Ye Not to Court?* (late 1522 and 1523). In it Skelton loosed against Wolsey the full strength of his fury. To this day, no one has discovered whether some particular event turned the poet furiously against the prelate, or whether the poem reflects the ever mounting feeling against Wolsey that finally led to his impeachment. In the end, Skelton may have gone too far, for the story that he had to seek sanctuary in Westminster to avoid the wrath of the Cardinal has never been disproved.[91]

From 1523, however, all Skelton's poems compliment Wolsey. His *Garland of Laurel*, published by Fawkes in October, 1523, contains an envoy addressed in high-sounding superlative to the Cardinal as well as the King: *"Ad serenissimam Majestatem Regiam, pariter cum Domine Cardinali, Legato a latere honorificatissimo, &c."* [92] But as late as May, 1523, a typical Skeltonic witticism—obviously aimed at the Cardinal's overreaching himself in church affairs—was enough a part of the public domain that Edward Hall in his *Chronicle* (15 Henry VIII) could quote the "merry poet":

And in this season, the Cardinall by his power legantine dissolued the Conuocation at Paules, called by the Archebishop of Cantorbury, and called hym and all the clergie to his conuocacion to Westminster, which was neuer seen before in Englande, wherof master Skelton, a mery Poet, wrote,

> *Gentle Paule, laie doune thy sweard:*
> *For Peter of westminster hath shauen thy beard.*[93]

It is hard to believe, then, that the poet's change was anything but formality. And surely he cannot be blamed for having made his peace with the most powerful prelate in the realm, who had caused even the formidable Duke of Buckingham to be executed

for treason, for no good reason except the Cardinal's personal
animosity.[94] (An eminent historian has suggested to me that the
second war with France in a decade caused even the old conservative aristocracy, the anti-Wolsey partisans, to unite behind
the King and Cardinal.[95])

Even before the end of 1522, Skelton may have placated the
Cardinal in some way, for he was free and away from London
by Christmas of that year. As the guest of the Countess of Surrey
(wife of the son of the Duke of Norfolk), the laureate spent
Christmas, 1522, at a castle in Yorkshire—Sheriff-Hutton, home
of the Duke of Norfolk. This castle, which once belonged
to the Neville family, the Earls of Westmoreland, had been
given by Henry VIII to Thomas Howard, Earl of Surrey and
hero of Flodden Field, in order to keep an eye on the northern
insurgents.[96] It was here in January, 1523, that Skelton began to
write his *Garland of Laurel*, the *apologia pro sua vita*—literarily
speaking—of which the opening scene takes place in the nearby
Forest of Galtres. The *Garland of Laurel* is generally non-political,
and its second envoy (addressed to King and Cardinal) reminds
Lord Thomas of the promised reward of a prebend made to the
poet: *"et fiat memor ipse precare / Prebendæ, quam promisit
mihi credere quondam."* [97]

There are strong echoes of this promise in a poem Skelton
wrote apparently at the Cardinal's request a few months later—
his lines on the "douty Duke of Albany." The second envoy to his
poem strikes a new note: "Skelton Laureat, Obsequious et Loyall,
to My Lorde Cardynals Right Noble Grace," reads the superscription; and the envoy reminds him of "Those wordes his grace
dyd saye / Of an ammas gray"—of a grey fur hood worn by those
who have prebends or by canons.[98] This office may have been the
bribe by which Wolsey bought him off—if, indeed, the recon-
ciliation came about in such a way.

Skelton's last known work, *A Replycacion agaynst Certayne
Yong Scolers*, contains a fulsome dedication in glowing terms to
"domino Thomæ . . . Cardinali meritissimo" from Skelton *laureatus*, who now "humilissimum dicit obsequium cum omni
debita reverentia." [99] The poem, a torrent of invective against
two young Cambridge heretics, represents more strongly than
any of the poet's work one of his most characteristic attitudes
—his deep and abiding hatred of the new Lutheranism. The trial

of one of the scholars, Thomas Bilney, was held in 1527 in the Chapter House at Westminster, very near Skelton's home; and since the poet shows a close acquaintance with the facts of the interrogation, it is likely that he was present when it was held. It is interesting to find, too, a "Magister Skelton" present at a trial of a Colchester fuller called Thomas Bowgas (May 4, 1528, at the London palace of the Bishop of Norwich), the circumstances of which were very similar to those of Bilney's trial the preceding year.[100]

A little more than a year after his appearance as witness in the Bowgas trial, Skelton died—on June 21, 1529. His death took place in Westminster, where he was living in peace, apparently, after having come to terms with Wolsey, who himself died in disgrace in November of the next year. According to the poet's early biographer Braynewode, Skelton was buried before the high altar at St. Margaret's, his parish church in Westminster, with this inscription on alabaster: "Ioannes Skeltonus vates pierius hic situs est" ("Here lies John Skelton, Pierian bard").[101] The stone and its legend have long since disappeared. But records still exist in the Churchwardens' Accounts of St. Margaret's of the expenses incurred for his funeral.[102] Four tapers were lighted for him and set around his corpse, and four torches illuminated his funeral procession. Church bells tolled for the dead priest, and a sum was paid for a special knell for him by Our Lady's Brotherhood, a parish guild of which Skelton was a member, along with many others attached to the neighboring palace. The old laureate's funeral, thus, appears to have been respectable without being flamboyant.

A record from Norwich on July 17, 1529, shows events moving along quite naturally in Diss. On that day, one Thomas Clark was appointed rector of Diss, a post left vacant by the natural death of the late rector, John Skelton ("per mortem naturalem magistri Johannis Skeltonne ultimi Rectoris eiusdem vacantem").[103] And the last known record of Skelton shows that William Mott (or Mote), curate of St. Margaret's, administered his estate.[104]

CHAPTER 2

Works

> *Quia difficile est*
> *Satiram non scribere.*

I *Westminster: Court of Henry VII*

a PROSE TRANSLATIONS

SKELTON'S literary output followed closely the events of his life. In other words, changes in subject matter and in literary style generally reflect changes in his social, religious, and political life and interests. The poet first became known—as Caxton points out—as a careful translator, not long after his undergraduate days. In his *Garland of Laurel,* he mentions several of his translations: "Of Tullis Familiars the translacyoun" and "Of Mannes Lyfe the Peregrynacioun." But he describes glowingly another work:

> Diodorus Siculus of my translacyon
>> Out of fresshe Latine into owre Englysshe playne,
> Recountyng commoditis of many a straunge nacyon;
>> Who redyth it ones wolde rede it agayne;
> Sex volumis engrosid together it doth containe. . . .[1]

The only one of these that has survived is the last—the *Historical Library* of Diodorus the Sicilian, translated from the Latin of Poggio Bracciolini (1380–1459).

The uniqueness of Skelton's translation has perhaps not been fully recognized. As the learned editors of his English translation of *Diodorus Siculus* explain, there was a great paucity of any Classics in English at the time Skelton was writing; and, except for Chaucer's translation of Boethius a century earlier, Skelton's translation of the first five books of *Diodorus* is the first such work of any length in the English language.[2]

Skelton's conventionality is everywhere to be seen in the *Dio-*

36

dorus, which is strictly in the rhetorical style of the later Middle Ages—the "aureate style." Basic to his work is the process of *amplificatio*—the art of expansion through the use of various rhetorical figures, fully explained by Geoffrey de Vinsauf in his *Poetria Nova,* a manual widely studied in medieval times. One finds in this early prose work all the rhetorical devices that Skelton made such astounding use of in his later works, transmogrified by his sharp wit and his special form of humor.

But the *Diodorus* was written when Skelton was a candidate for a degree in rhetoric—the laureation; and its aureate style, based upon expansion, dilation, amplification, is everywhere paramount. Nothing is stated simply: extreme tautology prevails, along with periphrasis, exaggeration, alliteration. Moreover, the "aureation" increases as the young rhetorician proceeds with his work, and "Skelton advances from a fumbling literalness in Book I to rolling periods in Book V." [3] The *Diodorus,* in fact, is an historical landmark in representing the peak of aureation. For although *amplificatio* remained a leading characteristic of Renaissance versification and prose style, never again was it to be found so unrestrained as one finds it here. Diffuseness is all; and to criticize Skelton for this diffuseness—as has sometimes been done[4]—is to denigrate him for the very thing that he aimed to achieve.

These lines about the god Mercury from Book I give a good idea of Skelton's early style in making his translation:

He was the first that espied the cause [course] of the sterris, and fonde the first practyck of musyke & armonye, of feates in wrastlynge, the caste of augrym [algarysme = arithmetic]; and for a curable remedye of bodyes diseased, he first fonde physyke & crafte of medecyne; the crafte & feate of harpynge, the feat of fydelynge with iij strynges. He fonde the thre seasons of the yere, by whos ordynary institucion he made thre partes appropred vnto melodyous armonye, that is to saye, treble, tenor, & mene. The treble hath his lusty proprete of somer; the tenor hath his baas proprete of the groos wynter; the mene toke his mesure & moderacion of thattemperat veer [springtime].[5]

How much Skelton developed in the course of this work may be seen in this typical passage from Book V—a bit a musical musings upon the Muses:

Vnto euerych one of thise ladies attributed is their offyce aptly of a
congruence vnto theym pertenynge in alle consideracions that vnto
the swete armonye of delectable musyke hath respecte, as touchynge
the melodyous prolacion of poemys, the lusty trypudacions [dancing
steps], wyth the roundes and daunces fulfyllyd with plesure. . . .
Vnto eche of thise Muses is asigned a name in specyal of their owne
propete whiche of eueryche of theym procedeth fructuously in efect.
. . . Dame Polinnya, so hight the seuenth, whos celestyal notes so
melodiously be entuned with musyke of so excellent swetenes, that she
rendryth the laureate glory of poetis in the ryall cyte of immortall
fame. . . . The nynthe, Caliope enscrybid is her name by occasion
that her surmountynge monocordis so proporcionatly, wyth the con-
tynued delectablenes of angelyk modulacion passynge alle other, ben
transcendynge.[6]

b ELEGIES

Skelton's translation of *Diodorus Siculus* was made sometime
before 1490 (when Caxton printed his *Eneydos*), possibly about
1485.[7] His earliest known poem, however, antedates that work
—an elegy on Edward IV, who died in 1483.[8] The poem, consisting of eight 12-line stanzas (three linked quartrains), is a
lament spoken by the young King himself, who long enjoyed the
favors of Fortune—"Where was in my lyfe such one as I, / Whyle
lady Fortune with me had continuaunce?"—but who now lies in
dust: *"Et, ecce, nunc in pulvere dormio!"* Each stanza ends with
this sad refrain. The King regrets some of his mistakes—"I storyd
my cofers and allso my chest / With taskys takynge of the
comenalte; / I toke ther tresure, but of her prayzeris mist"—and
asks forgiveness: "Whom I beseche with pure humylyte / For to
forgeve and have on me pety." He also lists some of his accomplishments:

> I made the Tower stronge, I wyst not why
> I knew not to whom I purchased Teterstall;
> I amendid Douer on the mountayne hye,
> And London I prouoked to fortify the wall;
> I made Notingam a place full royall,
> Wyndsore, Eltam, and many other mo. . . .

And he considers the vanity of it all: "Where is now my conquest
and victory? / Where is my riches and my royal aray / . . . .
As vanyte, to nought al is wandred away." Quite in the scholastic

tradition, he cites several great ones—Alexander the Great, "stronge Sampson," Solomon, Absalom—all of whom returned "vnto wormis mete." He ends by yielding, as all must do, to Death, and asks for the prayers of the people, "Humbly beseching thé, God, of thy grace! / O ye curtes commyns, your hertis vnbrace," while he, Edward, sleeps forever in dust: *"Et, ecce, nunc in pulvere dormio!"*

The elegy, then, is based upon an idea that informs much of the poetry of the later Middle Ages—*memento mori*, "all flesh is grass," the vanity of mortal existence. Skelton seems to have treated this topic at least once in a treatise in Latin or English; for in his *Garland of Laurel* he lists among his books, "Item to lerne you to dye when ye wyll," with a marginal note beside it citing a line from Horace: "Mors ultima linea rerum." [9] Whatever it may have been, the book has not survived, but the idea of death as the ultimate end of things recurs often in Skelton's verse.

Skelton, in fact, gives in stanza eight a source of the main ideas in his poem, as he asks, "Why should a man be proude or presume hye? / Sainct Bernard therof nobly doth trete." The reference is to the poem *De Contemptu Mundi*, attributed to Bernard of Cluny (1090–1153), which emphasizes the transitoriness of life, the inevitability of death, the return of man to ashes, and which bids man continually contemplate the thought of death. Some of Skelton's great names appear in St. Bernard's procession of famous ones from the past: "Dic, ubi Salomon, olim tam nobilis? / Vel ubi Samson est, dux invincibilis? / Vel pulcher Absalon, vultu miribilis?" [10]

Skelton's poem, moreover, although not strictly a dance of death, certainly echoes that tradition—imported from France and especially popular in literature, painting, sculpture, and glass, near the end of the fifteenth century.[11] Skelton's dead King, indeed, speaks of Lady Fortune as leading him a dance—the *danse macabre*. And so here Skelton has created something new: the combination of the idea of Fortune's fickleness and the death dance.

Rhetorically, as one might expect, the elegy is conventional in the use of many devices and figures taught in the schools.[12] To point out only a few of these, one finds much tautology ("I storyd my cofers and allso my chest"), alliteration ("Seyth a man is but a sacke of stercorry"), catalogues, exclamations ("O lady

Bes, longe for me may ye call!"), and questions. The Latin refrain
probably relates the poem to the *Vade mori* tradition. The use
of the Latin refrain also seems to emphasize a very definite relationship between Skelton and his great contemporary in the North,
William Dunbar (born c. 1460). The Scots poet had a fondness
for refrains, both in Latin and in the vernacular; and his poem
"Of Manis Mortalitie" is very similar, indeed, to Skelton's elegy.
Dunbar begins the poem with the command, *"Memento, homo,
quod cinis es!"* and ends each stanza with the refrain *"Quod
tu in cinerem reverteris."* [13] Skelton, too, opens with a command
—*"Miseremini mei!"*—as the dead king begs for pity, and closes
each stanza with the Latin refrain, *"Et, ecce, nunc in pulvere
dormio!"*

Most interesting of all, however, and the unmistakable mark
of Skelton laureate, is the handling of short and long syllables
exactly as in music. Although this poem is invariably said to be
written in rhyme-royal (having five beats to the line), many of
the lines actually have four strong beats—usually preceded by
an upbeat (weak); extra syllables are simply "divided"—as
quarter notes are divided into eighths and sixteenths—and made
to fit. The result is an eminently singable line, with strong beats
falling naturally upon the first note of each bar in 2/4 time: "She
toke me by the *hand* and *led* me a *daunce.*"

The elegy on the Earl of Northumberland ("Skelton Laureat
vpon the Doulourus Dethe and Muche Lamentable Chaunce of
the Most Honorable Erle of Northumberlande")[14] is a much
longer poem, written in the conventional rhyme royal—the seven-
line stanza of iambic pentameter rhyming *ababbcc*, supposedly
invented by Chaucer and used for much serious verse until well
into the Renaissance. Traditional rhetorical figures appear in the
elegy in full force: alliterative tautological expressions ("The
dedely fate, the dolefulle desteny"), abundant apostrophe ("O
Clyo . . . / Adres thé to me"), questions and *repetitio* ("What
shuld I flatter? What shuld I glose or paint?"), climax ("I wayle,
I wepe, I sobbe"), comparison with heroes of antiquity ("Lyke
to Aeneas," "Valiant as Hector"). The tone is the approved one
of studied modesty ("My wordes vnpullysht be, nakide and
playne, / Of aureat poems they want ellumynynge"). After
mourning for the Earl, the poet takes to task those who treach-
erously have murdered him:

> I say, ye comoners, why wer ye so stark mad?
>> What frantyk frensy fyll in your brayne?
> Where was your wit and reson ye should haue had?
>> What wilful foly made yow to ryse agayne
>> Your naturall lord? alas, I can not fayne. . . .

But he ascribes the Earl's death to "fykkell" Fortune's frown, to "Fortunes duble dyse." And near the end, the poet addresses himself to the Earl's successor (to whom he also addressed some Latin lines on the same subject):

> O yonge lyon, but tender yet of age,
>> Grow and encrese, remembre thyn estate;
> God thé assyst unto thyn herytage,
>> And geue thé grace to be more fortunate!

Finally, Skelton commends the Earl to the Virgin Mary and places him with the Holy Trinity, triumphant in heaven.

The laureate, then, becomes very personal in sentiment in his elegy, although the poem is usually spoken of as being quite conventional. This personal quality is especially strong in his concern over the future of the "young lion" and in the highly religious tone at the end of the poem. And, again, many of the lines (although supposedly in the pentameter of rhyme royal) are built upon a pattern of four strong beats with unstressed syllables shortened as necessary. The four beats are plain to hear, as, for example, in the line, "The *com*mons re*nyed* ther *tax*es to *pay*."

C EARLY LYRICS

From Skelton's early years, probably, comes a group of lyrics that have never been dated with any degree of accuracy. Written before Skelton entered the priesthood, in all likelihood, these poems have long been considered quite traditional. Through their traditional rhetoric, however, one may often see the essential Skelton emerging. Five of the poems were printed by Richard Pynson (no date: c. 1526) as *Dyuers Balettys and Dyties solacyous, deuysyd by Master Skelton, Laureat.*[15] The common factor here is that all the poems are love lyrics—although two or three of them might be considered love lyrics in reverse; and the tenderly

personal tone of several of them leads one to think that they may
have been written to some very definite lady.

The first of these, in Skelton's favorite four-beat meter, has a
charming opening line ("My darlyng dere, my daysy floure")
after the prophetic refrain, "With, Lullay, lullay, lyke a chylde,/
Thou slepyst to long, thou art begylde." But the poem is not a
lullaby: it shows the reverse side of the *carpe diem* idea. For the
lover, "All drowsy dremyng, dround in slepe," loses his lady
("She left hym slepyng, and stale away") and is properly dressed
down by the poet: "What dremyst thou, drunchard, drousy
pate! . . . / Behold, thou lyeste, luggard, alone! / Well may thou
sygh, well may thou grone. . . ."

No lilting refrain softens the next poem, which opens with the
slowly moving, heavy, five-stress line of the proper rhyme-royal
stanza. "The auncient acquaintance, madam, between vs twayn,"
states the poet, causes him to wish to describe the lady in conventional terms. But he is unable to do so because of a rumor,
"How in good horsmen ye set your hole delyght, / And haue for-
goten your old trew louyng knyght." Immediately, the horses take
over. The poet breaks into a trot, "Wyth bound and rebound,
bounsyngly take vp." And for three stanzas Skelton lets himself
go in a gallop of ribaldry, as he chides the wanton wife for her
actions while her "jentyll husband" is away fighting. This tor-
rential Philippic over, the poet returns to a mood of quietness,
and in the final stanza counsels the lady, "Play fayre play, ma-
dame, and loke ye play clene, / Or ells with gret shame your
game wylbe sene."

Impersonal and stylized is the poem beginning, "Knolege,
aquayntance, resort, fauour with grace." Each of its careful stanzas in strict rhyme royal dwells upon a different aspect of the
young lady to whom the verses are addressed. Her name appears
in the letters beginning each stanza: KATERYN. The poet describes
her spiritual qualities and compares her (in separate stanzas) to
refreshing waters, to various jewels, to a mirror.[16] Singing the
praises of this lady who is far away, the poet ends with a couplet
worthy of the Elizabethan sonneteers: "For I haue grauyd her
wythin the secret wall / Of my trew hart, to loue her best of all!"

A one-stanza rhyme-royal poem follows, first in Latin (*"Cuncta
licet cecidisse putas discrimina rerum"*), then in English: "Though
ye suppose all jeperdys ar paste." Here the poet warns "of For-

tunes dowble cast," and ends with a witty bit of *interpretatio:*
"That when ye thynke all daunger for to pas, / Ware of the
lesard lyeth lurkyng in the gras." A final short poem, beginning
"Go, pytyous hart, rasyd with dedly wo," plays upon the word
fortune and the idea of Fortune's unkindness to lovers. Closing
with a strong couplet, the poet takes what comfort he can: "But
Fortune enforsyth me so carefully to endure, / That where I loue
best I dare not dyscure." This poem is signed, "Skelton, laureat, At
the instance of a nobyll lady." One hopes the little poem with its
pitiful refrain ("That wher I loue best I dare not dyscure") was
great consolation to the noble lady.

The poem "To mastres Anne," beginning "Womanhod, wanton,
ye want," [17] obviously comes also from Skelton's years at the
court of Henry VII. In rhyme-royal stanzas, the poet berates
Mistress Anne—who once dwelt "at the Key in Temmys strete"
—for her promiscuousness. He plays upon the word *key*—"Youre
key is mete for euery lok, / Youre key is commen and hangyth
owte; / Youre key is redy, we nede not knok—" and, at the end,
bids her hold her tongue. Skelton may actually have had such a
friend living in Thames Street, for in his *Garland of Laurel* he
speaks of having written other poems to her:

> The vmblis of venyson, the botell of wyne,
>   To fayre maistres Anne that shuld haue be sent,
> He wrate therof many a praty lyne,
>   Where it became, and whether it went,
>   And how that it was wantonly spent;
> The Balade also of the Mustarde Tarte;
> Suche problemis to paynt it longyth to his arte.[18]

Throughout the *Garland of Laurel*, the marginal notes are especially interesting, oftentimes amusingly witty. Opposite this
stanza, Horace's famous dictum is humorously quoted: "Aut
prodesse volunt aut delectare poetae" (Poets wish to be either
useful or pleasing). The "Ballad of the Mustard Tart" has not
survived, but one can guess the type of poem it was since *mustard* was a euphemism very much a part of the erotic language
of the day.[19]

Perhaps another friend was called Margery. At any rate, Skelton devotes two entire stanzas to her in the *Garland,*[20] the first of
which runs,

> Of manerly maistres Margery Mylke and Ale;
>   To her he wrote many maters of myrthe;
> Yet, thoughe I say it, therby lyith a tale,
>   For Margery wynshed, and breke her hinder girth;
>   Lor, how she made moche of her gentyll birth!
> With, Gingirly, go gingerly! her tayle was made of hay;
> Go she neuer so gingirly, her honesty is gone away.

Only one of these "matters of mirth" has survived—"Manerly
Margery Mylk and Ale." [21] This piece, found in the famous collection of Tudor music called *The Fayrfax Book* in a setting by
William Cornish, is another tirade against the faithless flirt, expressed chiefly through the same ribald horse-and-rider figures
that are echoed in the stanza about Margery in the *Garland of
Laurel*. This poem, with a basically four-beat line (although it
purports to be in rhyme royal) has a ringing (("giddap") refrain
that is reduplicated in the final stanza—obviously owing to the
musical setting in which the refrain was repeated. The three-part
setting for bass, tenor, and mean is in the lightly imitative style
of the period. Skelton's words sing themselves. And the rhythmic
pattern of the music (beginning on an upbeat) easily follows the
words, as in the refrain:

> ¾ Gup *Christian Clowte*, gup, *Jak* of the *vale!*
>   With *Manerly Margery Mylk* and *Ale*.

d COURT SATIRES

In these mysogynistic lyrics, Skelton shows his attitude toward
the "querelle des femmes" as definitely as did his younger contemporary Rabelais a few decades later. Other aspects of court
and city life also angered Skelton, and provoked him to some of
his strongest satire. The first of these satires is a *sarcasmos* in
both English and Latin *Agaynst a Comely Coystrowne*, written
in late 1495 or early 1496.[22] This poem, unique among Skelton's
works, is couched almost entirely in musical terms. The *"comely
coystrowne"*—that is, handsome scullery-boy—*"that curyowsly
chawntyd, and curryshly cowntred, and madly in hys musykks
mokkyshly made agaynste the ix. Musys of polytyke poems and
poettys matryculat"* (who had, in other words, spoken out against
the laureate) is mercilessly satirized in musical terms for aiming
too high at court, for living above his station. A most musical line

sums up the situation: "For *Jak* wold be a *jentylman*, that *late* was a *grome*." If the satire is to be taken literally, the upstart courtier must have been a music teacher: "For lordes and ladyes lerne at his scole; / He techyth them so wysely to solf and to fayne, / That neyther they synge wel prycke songe nor playne." The "proud page"—who, in the Latin verses following the English, is called a "singing and organ-playing ass" [23]—is first held up to scorn (for his poor singing) in musical puns that became conventional in Renaissance poetry, puns on such words as *solfa* (singing by syllables); the voices *treble, bass, mean;* measure (or proportion—rhythmic terms); the syllable *mi;* discant (a counter melody to a given tune):

> He can not fynd it in rule nor in space:
>> He solfyth to haute, hys trybyll is to hy;
> He braggyth of his byrth, that borne was full bace;
>> Hys musyk withoute mesure, to sharp is hys my;
>> He trymmyth in hys tenor to counter pyrdewy; [24]
> His dyscant is besy, it is withoute a mene;
> To fat is hys fantsy, hys wyt is to lene.

And later, in much the same vein, "He fyndeth a proporcyon in his prycke songe, / To drynk at a draught a larg and a long—" such drinking being impossible, since "a large and a long" were two different note values. Pricksong, of course, means printed music with regular note values, as opposed to the traditional plainsong of the Church with its irregular rhythms.

The upstart—perhaps a Flemish knight newly arrived at court, possibly in the wake of the wool trade—is also taken to task in marvelously onomatopoeic verses for his lack of facility in playing musical instruments:

> He lumbryth on a lewde lewte, Roty bully joyse,
>> Rumbyll downe, tumbyll downe, hey go, now, now!
> He fumblyth in hys fyngeryng an vgly good noyse,
>> It semyth the sobbyng of an old sow.

"Roti bouilli joyeulx" [25] was a popular dance tune from Brabant in Flanders, where Skelton may have gone for his overseas laureation. The tune is mentioned in the anonymous fifteenth-century Scots poem, *Colkolbie Sow,* where there are many Flemish allusions, including a story about how Flanders got its name: here "sum" dance to one melody and "sum" to another: "Sum rusty bully w^t a bek." [26] It is probably not by accident that Skelton compares Jack's playing to the "sobbing of an old sow." Skelton mentions the tune about "jolly roast beef" again in *Magnificence*, when Courtly Abusion enters singing, "Rutty bully, ioly rutterkyn, heyda!" [27] Thus both "Roti bouilli" and the reference to Skelton's poem "Jolly Rutterkin" reinforce the idea of the Flemish knight ("rutterkin") who perhaps made his money in the wool trade and aped his betters at court.

Flemish overtones also appear in references to Perkin Warbeck and Martin Swart:

> Wyth, Hey, troly, loly, lo, whip here, Jak,
> Alumbek sodyldym syllorym ben!
> Curyowsly he can both counter and knak
> Of Martyn Swart and all hys mery men.
> Lord, how Perkyn is proud of hys pohen! [28]

There seems to have actually been a song about Martin, with a refrain similar to Skelton's line: "Martin swart and his man, sodledum sodledum, / Martin swart and his man, sodledum bell." [29] The "Hey trolly lolly" might be either a nonsense refrain or a reference to some particular song. Folly in *Magnificence* speaks of the foolish person in these same terms: "He dawnsys so longe, hey, troly loly, / That euery man lawghyth at his foly." [30] "Jolly Rutterkin" is an even stronger satire of the Flemish gallant ("rutterkin").[31] Like the poem against the musical upstart, it is strong mockery of the unpleasant characteristics of the "jolly rutterkin." Here it is not his musical and intellectual lacks that are held up to scorn, but his physical habits—of dressing, of eating, and of drinking. He is a sort of Grobianus: "Rutterkyn can speke no englissh / His tonge rennyth all on buttyrd fyssh / Besmerde with grece abowte his disshe / Like a rutter hoyda." Rutterkin's gross manners as described by Skelton, who probably had many opportunities to observe them, are quite similar to those associated with Flemings and High Dutch in *The Libel of English Policy*, written in 1436:

> Ye have herd that twoo Fflemmynges togedere
> Wol undertake, or they goo ony whethere,

Or they rise onys, to drinke a barelle fulle
Of gode berkyne; so sore they hale and pulle,
Undre the borde they pissen as they sitte;
This cometh of covenant of a worthy witte.[32]

Undoubtedly echoing popular sentiment, Skelton's poem was held in such esteem that it was set to music for three voices (bass, tenor, mean—the usual arrangement for men's voices) by his contemporary in Westminster, William Cornish.[33] With its reiterated refrain ("Like a rutter hoyday!") and many shouted *hoydays,* the piece must have caused the royal rafters to ring when sung at the top of their voices by Cornish's colleagues in the Royal Chapel.

All these poems—elegies, lyrics, satires—have been relatively short ones. Skelton's first extant long poem is the *Bowge of Courte,*[34] which satirizes a practice that Skelton must have found truly appalling—the abuse of royal favor. Taking its title from the customary phrase for free rations (*bouge*) at court, the poem was printed by Wynken de Worde before he moved from Westminster in 1500. In many respects, the poem is quite like the conventional allegory. Written in rhyme-royal stanzas, it is set in the dream framework, it opens with an astrological dating (when Virgo ruled the heavens, which may mean it was written in late August or September, 1498), and its characters are allegorical qualities. The poem is stylized, too, in its very careful divisions. There is a Prologue, followed by dialogue between the hero Drede (Modesty) and each of the seven passengers with him on the good ship *Bouge of Court:* Favell (Flattery), Suspicion, Harvy Hafter, Disdain, Riot, Dissimulation, and Deceit. The ship is owned by a "lady of estate," Dame Sanspeer; her merchandise, "ryche and fortunate," is Favour; her chief gentlewoman is Danger; and behind her throne is the legend *"Garder [gardez]le fortune, que est mauelz et bone!"*

The simple hero, Drede, who has "but small substaunce," comes to the lady to buy some of her ware, at which another gentlewoman, Desire, tells him that he must be aggressive ("Abasshe you not, but hardely be bolde"), lends him the jewel Bon Aventure, and reminds him that "Fortune gydeth and ruleth all oure shyppe." Once aboard, suing for Favour, Drede finds that the four and three "subtyll persones" also sailing on the ship will have

little to do with him. Favell, however, finally makes up to him,
denying his own personality: "I can not flater, I muste be playne
to thé." Suspicion comes next, distrustful of anyone he sees talk-
ing to Drede: "But I wonder what the deuyll of helle / He sayde
of me, whan he with you dyde talke." Drede becomes more and
more frightened ("I dare not speke, I promysed to be dome")
when the charming swindler, Harvy Hafter, "came lepynge,
lyghte as lynde."

Between speeches, Drede hears the other passengers planning
to toss him overboard. Disdain starts a conversation, to be interrupted by the noisy approach of Riot—"russhynge all at ones,"
whirling "a payre of bones." Riot comments on the fact that
Drede is a newcomer: "What arte thou? I sawe thé nowe but
late. / Forsothe, quod I, in this courte I dwell nowe." Riot
chatters to Drede of the joys of harlotry, after which he rushes
off "to the stewys syde," leaving Drede to Dissimulation, a fellow
with "faces tweyne," "a knyfe hyd in his one sleue" and a spoon
to feed fools in the other. His speech, too, is a compound of lies:
"I hate this faynynge, fye vpon it, fye!" Drede's story gets more
exciting, as he continues: "Sodaynly, as he departed me fro, /
Came pressynge in one in a wonder araye: / Er I was ware, be-
hynde me he sayde, Bo!" As Deceit spoke in Drede's ear of sub-
tlety and of craft, Drede noticed

> lewde felawes here and there
> Came for to slee me of mortall entente;
> And, as they came, the shypborde faste I hente,
> And thoughte to lepe; and euen with that woke,
> Caughte penne and ynke, and wrote this lytyll boke.

The poem that starts so conventionally, then, turns out to be
quite different from the usual dream allegory. In fact, in the
Prologue, Skelton has his hero lying in a quay-side inn, instead
of slumbering in a lovely bower: "At Harwyche Porte slumbrynge
as I laye, / In myne hostes house, called Powers Keye;" and the
background turns out to be nightmare rather than pleasant dream.
Instead of pleasant companions on the ship, the four and three
passengers compare very favorably in an unpleasant way with
their best known medieval cousins—the Seven Deadly Sins. Moreover, the good ship—"Her takelynge ryche and of hye apparayle"

(a line later quoted by Wordsworth in a sonnet)[35]—does not bring the hero to port: Drede is forced by his wicked companions to leap overboard for his life.

In characterization, Skelton is anything but conventional. From the entrance of Favell, who flatters excessively, each speaker dramatizes his own personality in approaching young Drede. But, as the poem moves along, Skelton loosens up and gives us wonderfully lively portraits of the charming rogue and the court roué. A change in style—a change to Skelton's own relaxed, musical lines—is responsible for this. The Harvy Hafter episode, for example, is far removed from the style of the opening stanza, with its careful pentameter line and astronomical language highly reminiscent of Chaucer:

> In autumpne, when the sonne *in Virgine*
>> By radyante hete enryped hath our corne;
> Whan Luna, full of mutabylyte,
>> As emperes the dyademe hath worne
>> Of our pole artyke, smylynge halfe in scorne
> At our foly and our vnstedfastnesse;
> The tyme whan Mars to werre hym dyde dres.

All this changes, as Harvy Hafter, a great lad for singing, rushes in: "His throte was clere, and lustely coude fayne / . . . And euer he sange, Sythe I am no thynge playne." He is constantly humming bits from popular tunes—"Hey, ho, rumbelow," "Row the boat, Norman," "Princess of youth." [36] And with a good Skeltonic four-beat swing, he laments the fact that he cannot read music (as a proper gentleman, of course, could do):

> Prynces of yougthe can ye synge by rote?
>> Or shall I sayle wyth you a felashyp assaye;
> For on the booke I can not synge a note.
>> Wolde to God, it wolde please you some daye
>> A balade boke before me for to laye,
> And lerne me to synge, Re, my, fa, sol!
> And, whan I fayle, bobbe me on the noll.

Riot, too, had his musical side: "And ay he sange, In fayth, decon thou crewe." But his real talents lay in the stews and alehouses ("He had no pleasure but in harlotrye"). Indeed, Riot's conversa-

tion is filled with much ribald horse imagery—quite similar to
that of Skelton's earlier Mistress Ann lyrics. Especially effective
is Skelton's musical line, "Counter he coude O *lux* vpon a potte"
—for the reference to the old hymn *O lux beata Trinitas*[37] tells
us at once that Riot does not know sacred music from profane
and that he sings hymn tunes in his carousing, beating a counterpoint with his tankard.

Skelton's *Bouge of Court,* then, is a sort of morality play in
reverse (like his *Elinor Rumming* some years later), in which
the conventional mingles with the highly individualistic. Ideas
exploited in the poem are concepts of the evils of court life, the
deadly sins, and the ship filled with rogues of various types. The
first two ideas had been part of the literary heritage for centuries. But the third one—to which Skelton was probably indebted for his ship—was a new departure, dating from 1494
when Sebastian Brandt's satire, *Das Narrenschiff* (well known
to the *res publica litterarum* in Locher's Latin translation of
1497), sailed into the mainstream of Western literature. The idea
of Fortune still prevails in Skelton's allegory ("But vnder hony
ofte tyme lyeth bytter gall") and French overtones are obvious.
At the end, Skelton spends only one stanza in pressing the moral.
"I wyll not saye it is mater in dede," he comments; "But yet oftyme
suche dremes be founde trewe: / Now construwe ye what is the
resydewe."

e RELIGIOUS LYRICS

Some half a dozen short religious poems are the product, too,
of Skelton's years at court. Several of them may have been inspired by deeply religious meditation and study preceding Skelton's entry into the priesthood. Although some critics have
doubted the authenticity of these poems, they are the subject
of a stanza in the *Garland of Laurel*, as Occupation, rehearsing
the poet's achievements, has this to say:

> With, Wofully arayd, and shamefully betrayd;
>   Of his makyng deuoute medytacyons;
> *Vexilla regis* he deuysid to be displayd;
>   With *Sacris solemniis*, and other contemplacyouns,
>   That in them comprisid consyderacyons;
> Thus passyth he the tyme both nyght and day,
> Sumtyme with sadnes, sumtyme with play.[38]

Skelton thus calls here by name two poems—"Woefully Arrayed"
and "Vexilla Regis"—and has three references to time (which
may or may not be significant: Skelton has a short poem "On
Time").

The first of these is a refrain poem,[39] with the line "Woffully
araid" (meaning here, as Dyce explains, "wofully disposed of or
treated, in a woful condition") ending each stanza, and with a
short stanza used as refrain at beginning and end of the poem:

> Woffully araid,
>> My blode, man,
>> For thé ran,
> It may not be naid;
>> My body bloo and wan,
> Woffully araid.

The irregular stanza after this refrain is built upon four lines
with internal rhymes, followed by three short rhyming lines (the
internal rhyme has been expanded to three), followed by a closing couplet and the refrain, "Woffully araid." Magnificent de-
scriptive powers combine with great depth of feeling to produce
such a stanza as this in which the crucified Saviour rehearses
the sufferings he has borne for mankind:

> Off sharpe thorne I haue worne a crowne on my hede,
> So paynyd, so straynyd, so rufull, so red;
> Thus bobbid, thus robbid, thus for thy loue ded,
> Onfaynyd not deynyd my blod for to shed;
>> My fete and handes sore
>> The sturdy nailis bore;
>> What myzt I suffir more
> Than I haue don, O man, for thé?
> Cum when thou list, wellcum to me,
>> Woffully araide.

This type of "composition of place" makes the poem, it would
seem, a striking forerunner of the so-called poetry of meditation
now associated with the Holy Sonnets of John Donne and later
writers.[40] The last two stanzas—corresponding to the analytical
and rationalistic parts of Donne's meditative pattern—express
infinite compassion for sinning mankind, as the Saviour pleads,

"But gyve me thyne hert fre to rewarde myn hyre." And the poem ends with a warning typical of Skelton (who at least once had a clergyman up before the ecclesiastical court, we recall, to answer for his soul's health): "Remember, man, thy sawlys helthe." Skelton must have had great satisfaction in hearing this piece performed in the Royal Chapel, for William Cornish made a four-part musical setting of it, which appears, along with other poems by the laureate, in *The Fayrfax Book*.[41]

Skelton's "Vexilla regis" [42] exploits virtually the same subject as "Woefully arrayed"—Jesus' ordeal of the Crucifixion and his love for mankind. In this poem, Skelton was obviously inspired by a well-known medieval hymn glorifying the Crucifixion, for he has taken as half of his refrain the incipit of the old hymn of Fortunatus (fl. 600) for the feast of the Holy Cross ("The King's banners go forth"):[43] "Now synge we, as we were wont, / *Vexilla regis prodeunt*." After the opening refrain, the first stanza takes its point of departure from the English version of the incipit of the old hymn:

> The kinges baner on felde is [s]playd,
> The crosses mistry can not be nayd,
> To whom our Sauyour was betrayd,
>   And for our sake;
> Thus sayth he,
> I suffre for thé,
>   My deth I take,
>   Now synge we, &c.

Although the crucified Saviour speaks throughout the poem, the point of view changes in the last stanza, and the poet himself appeals to Jesus for blessing:

> Now, Jesu, for thy great goodnes,
> That for man suffred great hardnes,
> Saue vs fro the deuyls cruelnes,
>   And to blys vs send,
> And graunt vs grace
> To se thy face
>   Withouten ende.
>   Now synge we, &c.

The obvious source of Skelton's rhyme-royal stanzas "On Time" [44] is the beautiful passage in the Old Testament (Ecclesiastes, III, 1–8), beginning, "To every thing there is a reason, and a time to every purpose under the heaven." Skelton opens with a couplet: "Ye may here now, in this ryme, / How euery thing must haue a tyme," and proceeds to philosophize upon time in terms of time's mutability ("Take tyme when tyme is, for tyme is ay mutable") as well as Ecclesiastes' idea of the differing occasions that make up life. He cites opposites in pairs, as does Ecclesiastes, some of them identical:

> Tyme to be sad, and tyme to play and sporte;
> Tyme to take rest by way of recreacion;
> Tyme to study, and tyme to use comfort;
> Tyme of pleasure, and tyme of consolation:
> Thus tyme hath his tyme of diuers maner facion;
> Tyme for to eate and drynke for thy repast;
> Tyme to be lyberall, and tyme to make no wast.

The moral tone is very strong: "And when tyme is, to holde thyselfe abacke; / For tyme well spent can neuer haue lacke." The highly lyrical concluding stanza takes a different view of time, expressing the idea of the changing seasons of the year, with emphasis upon winter:

> The rotys take theyr sap in tyme of vere;
> In tyme of somer flowres fresh and grene;
> In tyme of haruest men their corne shere;
> In tyme of wynter the north wynde waxeth kene,
> So bytterly bytynge the flowres be not sene;
> The kalendis of Janus, with his frostes hore,
> That tyme is when people must lyue vpon the store.

Among Skelton's early works are three very brief poems (of two stanzas each in rhyme royal) to the members of the Holy Trinity: "Prayer to the Father of Heauen," "To the Seconde Parson," and "To the Holy Gooste." [45] Each of these is a refrain poem, and each begins with an apostrophe, which is expanded by means of such conventional devices as repetition, alliteration, catalogue, climax, exclamation. Nonetheless, deep personal feeling

inevitably shines through: "Assyst me, good Lord, and graunte
me of thy grace, / To lyue to thy pleasure in word, thoughte,
and dede, / And, after this lyfe, to see thy glorious face." These
little poems are very probably among the "devote meditations"
and "other contemplations" that the aging laureate remembered
years later in his *Garland of Laurel.*

The refrain-line in the "Prayer to the Father of Heauen" is the
poet's entire thought "after this lyfe, to see thy glorious face."
The poem *"Vexilla regis"* ends with the same idea: "And graunt
vs grace / To se thy face / Withouten ende." These identical
lines also appear near the end of a short lyric "Vppon a Deedmans Hed":[46] "But graunt vs grace / To se thy face, / And to
purchace / Thyne heuenly place. . . ." According to Skelton's
superscription, this lyric "Upon a Deadman's Head" is a *"gostly
medytacyon in Englysh, couenable in sentence, comendable, lamentable, lacrymable, profytable for the soule"* upon a skull—
real or ornamental?—*"that was sent to hym from an honorable
jentyllwoman for a token."* This object sets up a *memento mori*
train of thought in the poet's mind—

> Youre vgly tokyn
> My mynd hath brokyn
> From worldly lust;
> For I haue dyscust
> We ar but dust,
> And dy we must—

and he proceeds, in emphatic short lines, to describe

> Deth holow eyed,
> With synnews wyderyd,
> With bonys shyderyd,
> With hys worme etyn maw,
> And his gastly jaw. . . .

Nothing can save us, he says, from mortality:

> Oure eyen synkyng,
> Oure bodys stynkyng,
> Oure gummys grynnyng,
> Oure soulys brynnyng.

But after this realistic *compositio,* the poet lifts his thought: "O goodly chyld," he pleads, "Of Mary mylde, / Then be oure shylde!" And he ends with the verses asking for grace "To se thy face . . . / Eternally / To beholde and se / The Trynyte!" Skelton cannot refrain from pointing up the moral for his "noble gentlewoman" and other such ladies with a short directive that echoes a book the lady might well have been familiar with—a medieval French allegory called the *Miroir des Dames.*[47] "*Myrres vous y,*" he says—"Look at yourselves therein." The reference, typically, is apt either for the token (the skull) or for the meditation inspired by it.

This lyric, then, reflects both the coming-of-death idea (shown in the earlier elegies) and the sustaining thought of eternal salvation, which, as we have seen, informs the short religious poems. Moreover, a recent critic has cogently argued that the meditation "Upon a Deadman's Head" is the first poem written in Skeltonics —in the short, clipped lines with a piling-up of rhymes that becomes characteristic later of the Skelton of Diss—and that the poem is a product of Skelton's court period rather than of a later time.[48] This argument becomes enormously strengthened when one observes that what the poet has actually done here is simply to construct an entire poem on the short-line pattern found so effective in "*Vexilla regis.*" The lines already cited—appearing in both poems—furnish the clue: "And graunt vs grace / To se thy face. . . ."

f SPECULUM PRINCIPIS

During his years as tutor to at least one little prince at the court of Henry VII, the laureate was busy writing tracts of an educational and moral nature. Several of these are mentioned in the *Garland of Laurel:*

> Of your oratour and poete laureate
> Of Englande, his workis here they begynne:
> *In primis* the Boke of Honorous Astate;
> Item the Boke how men shulde fle synne;
> Item Royall Demenaunce worshyp to wynne;
> Item the Boke to speke well or be styll;
> Item to lerne you to dye when ye wyll.
> . . . .

Item New Gramer in Englysshe compylyd.

·   ·   ·   ·   ·   ·   ·   ·   ·

And of Soueraynte a noble pamphlelet. . . .[49]

None of these works has survived, so far as is known. But another such work, written at Eltham on August 28, 1501 (as the author states at the end) and brought to light not many years ago, is emphasized in the *Garland:*

> The Duke of Yorkis creauncer [tutor] whan Skelton was,
>   Now Henry the viij. Kyng of Englonde,
> A tratyse he deuysid and browght it to pas,
>   Callid *Speculum Principis,* to bere in his honde,
>   Therin to rede, and to vnderstande
> All the demenour of princely astate,
> To be our Kyng, of God preordinate.[50]

This work is Skelton's "Mirror of a Prince," rededicated and presented to Henry in 1509 after the prince had become King.

"Skelton, laureate, once his most humble tutor" ("quondam suus humillimus didasculus"), begins his treatise with a florid dedication to his erstwhile pupil. A page or two is missing at the beginning of the tract, but the first of the homily is a lecture on virtue, held up traditionally as the most prominent characteristic of the ideal prince. Virtuous Romans are cited as examples of highly virtuous heroes, and the lecturer concludes this part: "It is my opinion, therefore, that princes should conduct their lives rather by the unfading glory of virtue than the vain pride of riches." In typical scholastic fashion, authorities are cited to support this opinion: Cato, Scipio, Horace, and "Aristotle *ad Alexandrum.*"

The rest of the treatise is for the most part a collection of maxims and precepts in *Reimprosa*—short, riming phrases of parallel prose. This rhetorical figure called "like ending" (*homoisteleuton*) was a favorite with medieval poets, and was occasionally badly overused by medieval preachers.[51] Such staccato phrases as these, taken from the *Speculum principis* and set on separate lines, become a strong and obvious ancestor of the type of verse for which Skelton is celebrated—the Skeltonic:

Habes consiliarios,
scios aut nescios.

. . . .

Noli nuptias temerare.
Virgines noli deflorare.
Viduas noli violare.

. . . .

Diu delibera.
Loquere pauca.

Those who have found the *Speculum* only a dull, pre-humanistic
moral tract[52] have surely missed the twinkle in the laureate's eyes
as he penned those lines! For after advising his pupil about his
counselors, he bids the lad not to dishonor his marriage, not to
deflower maidens, not to violate widows, to think a long time and
to speak little. In the light of the events of history, this advice
was ironic indeed.

II *Diss*

a MOCK ELEGIES

The poems produced by Skelton during his years at Diss were
anything but the meditations and contemplations that readers
familiar with his early religious poems might expect. Sometimes
whimsical, occasionally bitter, always sardonic—this is the Rector
of Diss, plagued by parishioners and Bishop alike, if we may
believe local accounts of him. The two major poems from this
epoch are *Philip Sparrow* and *Ware the Hawk*. But before these,
he tried his hand at a couple of mock epitaphs for two rather
obnoxious members of his flock. A short prelude sets the tone for
this hilarious postmortem:

This tretise devysed it is
Of two knaues somtyme of Dis.
Though this knaues be deade,
Full of myschiefe and queed,
Yet, where so euer they ly,
Theyr names shall neuer dye—

and then the poet names the objects of his satire: "*Compendium
de duobus versipellibus, John Jayberd, et Adam all a knaue,*

deque illorum notissima vilitate" ("A short account of two sly
fellows, John Jaybeard and Adam All-a-knave, and of their notorious meanness").[53] There follows first "A Deuoute Trentale
[thirty masses for the dead] for Old John Clarke, Sometyme the
Holy Patriarke of Dis" in mocking macaronics, Latin and English.
The date (1506) of old John's death is given: *"Obiit sanctus iste
pater / Anno Domini MD. sexto,"* along with a character sketch:
"In malitia vir insignis, / Duplex corde et bilinguis." And Skelton
ends the first section: *"Sepultus est* amonge the wedes: / God
forgeue hym his mysdedes!"

The next section of the poem is a

> *Dulce melos*
> *Penetrans cœlos*

consisting of Latin hexameters about old John—apparently what
the heavenly choirs sing when John appears for admission:
"Carmina cum cannis / cantemus festa Joannis. . . ."[54] To the
question, *"Quid petis, hic sit quis?"* (What do you want, who
might this be?) the answer is "John Jaybeard, inhabitant of Diss,
who was continually mixed up in quarrels and lawsuits while he
was alive."

A final burst of macaronics, beginning *"Jam jacet hic* starke
deed, / Neuer a toth in his heed," entombs old John. At the end,
the mock-eulogist mingles bits of sailor-songs with the Doxology
("World without end, Amen") heard so often in the liturgy of
the Church: "Wit[h], hey, howe, rumbelowe, / *Rumpopulorum, /
Per omnia secula seculorum! Amen."* A brief Requiem is then to
take place (words not given), and Skelton brings to an end his
"devotum trigintale": "Vale Jayberd, valde male!"

The epitaph for Adam Uddersall follows immediately in the
manuscript copied out in 1507 (when Skelton was probably visiting in Cambridge) by the Vicar of Trumpington:

> Adam Vddersall,
> *Alias dictus* Adam all
>   a knaue, his
> Epitaph foloweth deuoutly;
> He was somtime the holy
>   Baillyue of Dis.

Short rhyming Latin verses castigate Adam for his misdeeds and wickedness, the same rhyme occurring eighteen times. And Adam is written off with a final non-blessing: "Belsabub his soule saue, / *Qui jacet hic*, like a knaue! . . ." Anyone who will take the trouble to follow Skelton through this torrent of Latin invective can see why his theological friend in Cambridge wished to preserve these examples of the laureate's tongue-in-cheek wit and copied them out. High tables in Cambridge halls must indeed have relished such savory bits as these!

Quite serious and filled with genuine compassion is another short poem from the year 1507—the "Lamentatio Urbis Norvicensis" [55]—when Norwich suffered two dreadful fires. In it Skelton simply laments the fate of the once beautiful city, now lying in ashes. The poem ends on a note of compassion: *"Urbs miseranda, vale! sors miseranda tua est"* (Farewell, city to be pitied; to be pitied is your fate).

b PHILIP SPARROW

Skelton's fondness for the mock elegy was not limited to poems about people. One of his most celebrated poems, *The Boke of Phyllyp Sparowe*,[56] immortalizes the pet bird of a young neighbor, Jane Scrope, who was a boarder at a convent run by Benedictine nuns just outside of Norwich. The bird's pretty, clever ways that so pleased its little mistress are ingeniously described in clipped, staccato verses calculated to make one see the small bird hopping about:

> Somtyme he wolde gaspe
> Whan he sawe a waspe;
> A fly or a gnat,
> He wolde flye at that;
> And prytely he wold pant
> Whan he saw an ant;
> Lord, how he wolde pry
> After the butterfly!
> Lord, how he wolde hop
> After the gressop!
> And whan I say, Phyp, Phyp,
> Than he wold lepe and skyp,
> And take me by the lyp.

But one day, alas, Phip had his moment of truth with "Gyb our cat"—and the poet's consolation gift for sorrowing Jane has made Phip one of the best known birds in English literature.

Philip's entombment in Skeltonics took place around 1508, for Alexander Barclay, in his very serious *Ship of Fools,* published in 1509, speaks slightingly of this sort of levity:

> I write no ieste ne tale of Robin Hood,
> Nor sowe no sparkles ne sede of viciousnes,
> Wise men loue vertue, wilde people wantonnes,
> It longeth not to my science nor cunning,
> For Philip the Sparrow the Dirige to singe.[57]

Skelton's poem falls into four distinct parts: two large divisions, each having two parts. First of all comes the elegy for Phip, which begins most aptly with the burial service and proceeds to a Mass of the Birds—a type of mock requiem with antecedents reaching far back into the Middle Ages.[58] This section of the poem is actually an early example of the stream-of-consciousness technique, as Jane ruminates about her pet. Bits of the Requiem Mass and the Office for the Dead float through her head (her own stepfather had been beheaded not long since), and she sings these. In fact, Jane begins her lament with the opening word of the antiphon for Vespers of the Office for the Dead, *Placebo Domino in regione vivorum.* This incipit, together with the first word of the response to it (*Dilexi quoniam, exaudiet Dominus vocem orationis meae*), is quite plainly sung by Jane, for not only are the words divided into syllables, but the musical syllables are given: "*Pla ce bo,* / Who is there, who? / *Di le xi,* / Dame Margery; / Fa, re, my, my."

Other phrases from the Office occur to Jane, as she recalls Phip's charming little ways and the great pleasure she took in him. But her lament is interrupted for a moment by a curse on all cats and "That cat specyally / That slew so cruelly / My lytell prety sparowe / That I brought vp at Carowe." Suddenly, Jane thinks of the solemn chant, "Lord, have mercy upon us!": "*Kyrie, eleison,* / *Christe, eleison,* / *Kyrie, eleison.*" And she brings her little service to an end, quite properly, with the Lord's Prayer: "For Phylyp Sparowes soule, / Set in our bederolle, / Let vs now whysper / A *Pater noster.*"

The second section of the poem marks a quick transition from the Office of the Dead to the Mass of the Birds—surely a natural idea in the mind of a young girl mourning the death of her pet sparrow. And a line from the Psalm of the Office marks the turn: *"Lauda, anima mea, Dominum!"* (Praise the Lord, O my soul!). The praising is done by a huge choir of birds, and along with each one goes a bit of information about his specialty as a singer. Of "robyn redbrest," says the poet,

> He shall be the preest
> The requiem masse to synge,
>
> . . . .
> The rauyn, called Rolfe,
> His playne songe to solfe;
>
> . . . .
> The popyngay to tell her tale,
> That toteth oft in a glasse,
> Shal rede the Gospell at masse;
> The mauys with her whystell
> Shal rede there the pystell.
> But with a large and longe
> To kepe iust playne songe,
> Our chaunters shalbe the cuckoue,
> The culuer, the stockedowue,
> With puwyt the lapwyng,
> The versycles shall syng.
>
> . . . .
> The pecocke so prowde,
> Because his voyce is lowde,
> And hath a glorious tayle,
> He shall syng the grayle [gradual].

A long line of birds will give out money to the poor: "That shall be theyr charge." And the poet, probably remembering many of his associates who could not sing at all, excludes the "estryge" from singing: "The best that we can, / To make hym our belman, / And let hym ryng the bellys; / He can do nothyng ellys." Bits of the plainsong of the Requiem keep recurring to Jane, and again the musical syllables are given along with the words: *"Requiem æternam dona eis, Domine!* / Fa, fa, fa, my, re, re."

As the burial service ends, Jane begins to think of a suitable epitaph for Phip, and she remembers all the books she has read:

> An epytaphe I wold haue
> For Phyllyppes graue:
> But for I am a mayde,
> Tymerous, halfe afrayde,
> That neuer yet asayde
> Of Elyconys well,
> Where the Muses dwell;
> Though I can rede and spell,
> Recounte, reporte, and tell
> Of the Tales of Caunterbury,
> Some sad storyes, some mery—

and many others. In this part of the poem Skelton gets in some comments about three of the best-known writers in the centuries immediately preceding his own. Gower is praised for "matter," not style: "Gowers Englysh is olde, / And of no value told; / His mater is worth gold, / And worthy to be enrold."
Chaucer is praised unstintingly:

> His mater is delectable,
> Solacious, and commendable;
> His Englysh well alowed,
> . . . .
> Chaucer, that famus clerke,
> His terms were not darke,
> But plesaunt, easy, and playne;
> No worde he wrote in vayne.

Lydgate, too, is given his due:

> Also Johnn Lydgate
> Wryteth after an hyer rate;
> . . . .
> No man that can amend
> Those maters that he hath pende;
> Yet some men fynde a faute,
> And say he wryteth to haute.

The Latin epitaph for the dead bird follows—in simple Latin— "*Flos, volucrum formose, vale! / Philippe, sub isto / Marmore jam recubas, / Qui mihi carus eras,*" signed by Skelton, "*Per me laurigerum / Britonum Skeltonida vatem,"* and ending with a charming tribute to Jane herself: *"Candida Nais erat, / Formosior ista Joanna est; / Docta Corinna fuit, / Sed magis ista sapit."* This section concludes with the whimsical line asking that the poet be remembered: *"Bien men souient"* (*Bien m'en souvient*).

The third long section of the poem has a title: "The Commendacions." Parodying the *Commendatio Animae* of the burial service, where the soul of the departed is commended to God with the reading of Psalms 117 and 118, Skelton plays on the word and writes a commendation not for Philip's soul but for Jane's beauty. He begins by chanting a couplet in Jane's honor: *"Beati im ma cu la ti in via, / O gloriosa fœmina!"* (Blessed are the undefiled in the way, O glorious woman!). The second line of this, obviously modeled upon the medieval hymn incipit, "O gloriosa Domina," becomes the refrain for the Commendations. In fact, Skelton relates this section to the breviary by using throughout a refrain-pattern, consisting of two lines (*"Hac claritate gemina / O gloriosa fœmina"*), followed by a second couplet composed of one line from Psalm 118 and another line from some other suitable Psalm or hymn.

The larger part of the Commendations is a detailed description of Jane, in the pattern set up by Geoffrey de Vinsauf in his *Poetria Nova.*[59] Jane's beauties are catalogued from her head to her feet, and after these her clothes:

> Wherto shuld I disclose
> The garterynge of her hose?
>
> . . . .
>
> Her kyrtell so goodly lased,
> And vnder that is brased
> Such plasures that I may
> Neyther wryte nor say. . . .

In line with tradition, the poet concludes by admitting that he cannot do justice to Jane's beauties:

> My pen it is vnable,
> My hand it is vnstable,
> My reson rude and dull
> To prayse her at the full;

and after one final statement of the refrain—*"Hac claritate gemina / O gloriosa fœmina!"*—he connects the Commendations with the Requiem Mass once again. For he quotes the beginning of the Introit of the Mass for the Dead, *"Requiem aeternam dona eis, Domine!"* and follows this by the incipit of the final oration of the *Commendatio Animae* in the service (*"Tibi, Domine, commendamus animam famuli tui"*).

This section ends with a defense of his "treatyse," asking that no one take offense at it: "Wherefore shulde I be blamed, / That I Jane haue named, / And famously proclamed?" His only excuse, he says, is Jane herself: "She is worthy to be enrolde / With letters of golde." Having said this in English and French (*"Car elle vault"*), Skelton repeats it in Latin hexameters, again signing his name.

Skelton's fears that some would take offense at his poem were apparently well founded, for he was later impelled to make "an adicyon" with some verses of explanation. He begins by stating a fact applicable to all ages: "The gyse now a dayes / Of some ianglynge iayes / Is to discommende / That they cannot amend." And he answers those who "depraue / Phillip Sparowes graue": "His *Dirige*, her Commendacyon / Can be no derogacyon, / But myrth and consolacyon / Made by protestacyon." Why should Jane be shamed by the poem? "I conjure thé, Phillip Sparow," the poet now bursts forth, "By Hercules that hell dyd harow"— and by a vast catalogue of the inhabitants of the underworld of Classical antiquity, followed by some characters from the Old Testament—

I coniure Phylyp, and call
In the name of kyng Saul
. . . .
That thou shortly tell,
And shew now vnto me
What the cause may be
Of this perplexite!

In the end, Skelton can only repeat in amazement (and in Latin) his question: How can anyone from spite condemn the holy rites of a sparrow!

In *Philip Sparrow*, as in his other mock elegies, Skelton follows the paths set long ago by the Goliardic poets[60]—medieval clerics

who roamed about and wrote rebellious satire generally, parodying the Mass, singing of love and of good wine, and changing
hymns to the Virgin into hymns to Venus. Perhaps Skelton's
Goliardic tendencies are what offended. For although the clever
poem entombing the bird and immortalizing the little girl seems
innocuous enough today, it was thought to be highly irreverent
in its own time by at least some of the orthodox clergy. Alexander Barclay was obviously not the only one who considered it
so "wanton," so light, as to be beneath notice. And Skelton was
not only enraged enough to write the epilogue in his own defense; many years later, in the *Garland of Laurel*, he devoted an
entire stanza to it:

> Of Phillip Sparow the lamentable fate,
>   The dolefull desteny, and the carefull chaunce,
> Dyuysed by Skelton after the funerall rate;
>   Yet sum there be therewith that take greuaunce,
>   And grudge therat with frownyng countenaunce;
> But what of that? hard it is to please all men;
> Who list amende it, let hym set to his penne.[61]

At this point, the entire epilogue to *Philip Sparrow* is inserted
verbatim in the *Garland of Laurel*. Although Skelton has included several lyrics to various ladies associated with Sheriff-
Hutton Castle in the *Garland*, he has not quoted at length from
any of his long poems except the *Dirige* for Philip. One can see
that its reception still rankled—and why would it not do so?—
after all those years.

Whatever Skelton's contemporaries may have thought of his
poem, modern critics agree that his intention was nowhere to
burlesque the Roman services for the dead. Instead, the poet has
worked with several literary traditions but has ended by producing something new and delightful of his own. Far from mocking the Mass and Office, he has introduced chants from the Requiem in a unique way to give point and depth to his elegy.[62]
Quite unusual is the way that he has divided his words into syllables and in some instances has even written out the musical
syllables, so that no reader can fail to realize that the reference
is to the plainsong of Mass and Office.

Reflected in the poem, too, is the popular medieval genre, the
titulus—memorial verses commemorating the dead and consoling

the living.[63] Attached to rolls of the dead—a listing on parchment of all the members of a religious community who had died during the year—and circulated from one monastery to another, this type of verse had become independent enough before Skelton's time to be parodied by monks of the later Middle Ages. Skelton's parody of the *titulus*, quite in the Goliardic tradition, underlines again the funereal aspects of the poem.

In *Philip Sparrow* there are, of course, overtones of Ovid and Catullus, each of whom wrote elegies on beloved pet birds.[64] And there is the Bird Mass—in connection with which one thinks at once of Chaucer—with Skelton, however, separated from the courtly love tradition and put to funeral use. Finally, there is the medieval tradition of *amplificatio* or expansion—seen especially in Jane's commendation. But here again, Skelton's humor and originality are asserted, as the poet devotes many lines of praise not only to her beauty but to the "warte vpon her cheke."

The poem, then, is typically Skeltonic in being an imaginative assimilation of old elements into something new and unique. It is informed at the same time by the poet's deep feeling for Jane, fondness for birds (still one of the most characteristic traits of the British), erudition, and impatience with stupidity. No wonder that Coleridge could call "Old Skelton's 'Philip Sparrow' an exquisite and original poem."

C WARE THE HAWK

The Rector of Diss might introduce bits of the funeral service into an elegy to set up the proper overtones. But it was another thing altogether to see an altar consecrated to God desecrated and its sacred appointments dunged upon by falcons. Yet this is what happened in his own church at Diss when a "lewd curate," a "parson benefyced," brought his hawk into the church and turned it loose to hunt. Skelton's scathing *Ware the Hauke*[65] was the result of witnessing this abuse. This time, however, the poet took nothing for granted: he carefully prepared for the poem's favorable reception. His opening verses make this clear: "This worke deuysed is / For such as do amys". And the purpose of the poem is stated even more clearly a few lines later:

> This boke we haue deuysed,
> Compendiously comprysed,

> No good priest to offende,
> But suche dawes to amende,
> In hope that no man shall
> Be myscontent withall.

Skelton then describes the scene in all its hideousness: "As priest vnreuerent, / Streyght to the sacrament / He made his hawke to fly, / With hogeous showte and cry."

Hearing all the commotion in the church, as hawks hunted and falconer swore, the Parson of Diss went up to investigate: "The church dores were sparred, / Fast boltyd and barryd, / Yet wyth a prety gyn / I fortuned to come in." [66] When taken to task by Skelton, the sporting parson paid no heed at all: "He sayde he would not let / His houndis for to fet, / To hunte there by lyberte / In the dyspyte of me." The commotion grew worse, as everything crashed around them:

> Downe went my offerynge box,
> Boke, bell, and candyll,
> All that he myght handyll;
> Cros, staffe, lectryne, and banner,
> Fell downe on this manner.

Devoted and orthodox son of Mother Church that he was, the enraged Rector of Diss had the visiting parson up before the ecclesiastical court: "But who so that lokys / In the officiallis bokis, / Ther he may se and reed / That this is matter indeed." However, "mayden Meed" [bribery] "Made theym to be agreed, / And so the Scrybe was feed / . . . And of the spiritual law / They made but a gewgaw."

Thus, having seen the records erased and the sinning cleric go unpunished, the Rector of Diss is driven to sing a bitter strain that rises to a full-scale symphony in such later works as *Colin Clout*: "The church is thus abused, / Reproched and pollutyd; / Correccion hath no place, / And all for lacke of grace." The offending clergyman is then compared to the great tyrants of history in a catalogue ranging from Diocletian to Zorobabel (and including—for the rhyme, one supposes—"cruel Jesabell"). Even such heathens as the Sultan and the Turk, thunders the poet, "Wrought neuer suche a worke, / For to let theyr hawkes fly / In the Church of Saint Sophy."

If canon law failed to take care of the sporting parson, Skelton laureate succeeded in anathematizing him magnificently in a final torrent of macaronic verse. Here the offender is repeatedly addressed in a most derogatory fashion as "Domine Dawcocke!" [jackdaw, fool], while the refrain "Ware the hawke!" gives unity to the diatribe. But the poet's sense of humor has now got the better of his anger, and the satire is lightened by witty little wordplays—like the perpetual pun on the word *hoc* (hawk): *Cave* [beware] *hoc,* / Doctor Dawcocke!" Many years later, Robert Greene was to echo this epithet in his play *Friar Bacon and Friar Bungay* (II, iv), where the scholar Miles speaks in Skeltonics, ending, "*Quid dicis ad hoc* [What say you to this] / Worshipful *Domine* Dawcock?"

Actually, Skelton's wry humor has lightened some of the most bitter and angry lines earlier in the poem, as he puns in two languages and in different aspects of being. One witty example is his way of saying that hawking had no place in the service by referring to the "Sarum use" (*secundum Sarum*), the pattern for the liturgical plainsong set by Salisbury Cathedral and followed throughout most of England: "On Sainct John decollacion [St. John's Eve] / He hawked on this facion, / *Tempore vesperarum,* / *Sed non secundum Sarum*" (at the time of Vespers, but not according to the Sarum use).

Who was the sporting parson who so aroused the Rector of Diss? The poet tells us near the beginning: "He shall be as now nameles, / But he shall not be blameles, / Nor he shal not be shameles." But at the end of the poem the lines, "Masyd, wytles, smery smyth, / Hampar with your hammer vpon thy styth," have led to tentative identification—a neighboring parson named Smith.[67] In the brief Latin *sarcasmos* that follows the English poem, Skelton calls his victim "*Rector de Whipstok*" and "*dominus Wodcock.*" Skelton's "tabull playne"—the enigmatic lines introduced to show up the "pekysh parsons brayne"—apparently puzzled other readers, as well as the one addressed, until Henry Bradley solved the mystery in 1896 and found a typical Skeltonic signature, in which the poet modestly proclaimed himself Britain's phoenix: "Sic, velut est Arabum phenix avis unica tantum / Terra Britanna suum genuit Skeltonida vatem." [68]

Ware the Hawk seems, at first glance, almost independent of its structure; for the entire outburst, after a *prologus,* is neatly divided into sections, each headed by a Latin imperative: *Observate, Considerate, Deliberate, Vigilate, Deplorate, Divinitate, Reformate, Pensitate*. "These commands state simply what clerics *ought* to do," says a recent critic.[69] This interpretation is perhaps true, but there is more to it than the moral implications. Skelton never mentions these commands, and yet the heading of each section seems amazingly apt, as one reads closely beneath it. For instance, *Vigilate* [be on guard against] heads the section that tells about the scribe bribed to destroy court records; *Reformate* heads the list of tyrants with an appropriateness too obvious for comment; and *Pensitate* is followed by the "tabull playne," which must have given the erring parson much to ponder for many years—and so with the others. Basic to the entire poem, indeed, is a structural principle that gives it an added dimension—the motet technique of medieval music. For marvelously analogous to this technique is Skelton's diatribe against Doctor Dawcock, which furnishes a running counterpoint in quick notes to the more sustained notes of the *cantus firmus* beneath, represented by the solemn Latin imperatives. Both parts, taken together, make one harmonious whole. And only a genius like Skelton, thoroughly familiar with music, could have brought it off.

III *Westminster: Court of Henry VIII*

a POLITICAL POEMS

Skelton's appointment as royal orator came, we recall, in 1512 or 1513. War with France was imminent and became an actuality in the summer of 1513; and war with the Scots resulted in the great Battle of Flodden Field on September 9, 1513. Aside from his Latin epitaphs honoring the royal sleepers in Westminster's Lady Chapel, proudly displaying his new title of *orator regius*, all of Skelton's poems at this time reflect these great political events.[70]

The first of these was the Latin ode of triumph modeled upon the well-known processional hymn of Fortunatus, *Salve, festa dies,* and celebrating Henry's victories (Tournai, Thérouenne) in France. This eulogy has the interesting superscription: *Chorus de Dis, &c. super triumphali victoria contra Gallos, &c. cantavit solemniter hoc elogium in profesto Divi Johannis ad Decollationem*[71]—that is, the hymn was sung on August 28, the Eve of the Feast of St. John. Beginning, "*Salve, festa dies, toto memorabilis*

ævo, / Qua rex Henricus Gallica bella premit" (Hail, festive day,
memorable for all eternity, because King Henry has put down
the Gallic wars), it eulogizes the King in sixteen hexameter lines.
There is no indication as to who composed the music for this
ode of triumph. It seems very likely that Skelton's choir—com-
prising the best singers in all England, those of the Royal Chapel
who came to France with Henry—sang the new words to older
music. Since polyphonic settings of *Salve, festa dies* had existed
for years, it would have been a relatively simple matter for any
trained musician to adapt one of these to the words of the royal
orator.

The triumphal ode must have been well received indeed. For
less than a month later, Skelton produced another such hymn,
again based on *Salve, festa dies,* but this time celebrating victory
over the Scots. Again, the superscription is highly informative:
*Chorus de Dis contra Scottos cum omni processionali festivitate
solemnisavit hoc Epitoma XXII die Septembris, &c.*[72] On this
festive occasion, Skelton's hymn was sung in a solemn procession,
an important part of the celebration during which Henry's gorgeous Cloth-of-Gold tent was set up, his private chapel sang
Mass and the *Te Deum,* and Bishop John Fisher quite properly
preached on the death of King James of Scotland. Skelton too,
announced in his opening lines the death of James: *"Salve, festa
dies, toto resonabilis ævo, / Qua Scottus Jacobus, obrutus ense,
cadit"* (Hail, festive day, echoing through the ages, for James of
Scotland, killed by the sword, has fallen.). And, having heaped
shame upon the Scots and glory upon the English, he ends on
a fittingly pious note, couched in musical metaphor: "England,
lead the chorus; let your drums and harps resound. Give praise
to the Lord, give holy prayers to God!"

When the Battle of Flodden Field was fought, however, it was
not known at first whether James had survived the slaughter or
not. Skelton's immediate response to news of victory was his
Ballade of the Scottysshe Kynge, a rather brief poem, beginning
"Kynge Jamy, Jomy your Joye is all go / Ye sommoned our kynge
why dyde ye so."[73] Printed by Richard Fawkes at once (1513),
this jubilation over the defeat of James has the honor of being
the earliest known, printed ballad in English literature. In this
poem the fate of the Scottish King is ambiguous, but the inge-

nious *orator regius* allowed for all emergencies in his verses: "For
to the castell of norham / I vnderstonde to soone ye cam, / For
a prysoner there now ye be / Eyther to the deuyll or the trinitie."

There is no mention of Flodden in the poem, which seems to
have been hastily composed as soon as the first letter from the
victorious Earl of Surrey had been received by the Queen and
sent by her to France. Skelton's processional *Epitoma* sung at the
Cloth-of-Gold celebration on September 22 shows much more
knowledge of the events of the battle, and was evidently written
after a second and more detailed letter from Surrey had reached
the King. The *Ballade*, in fact, deals for the most part—like the
opening lines—with a famous episode that took place when
James sent a herald to "summon" Henry home; and the poem
was probably the first account of this arrogant act, an account
later copied by Hall and other historians. Both the King and his
loyal orator regarded the "summoning" as an altogether disgraceful proceeding.[74]

Sometime after September 19 (when a copy of Surrey's second
letter reached Henry, together with the dead King's gauntlet and
a piece of his plaid coat), Skelton expanded his brief *Ballade of
the Scottysshe Kynge* into a torrent of invective *Against the
Scottes.*[75] In staccato half-lines he gloats over the fact that
"Jemmy is ded / And closed in led." With a shift in rhythm, he
is gleeful at thought of the battle: "Continually I shall remember
/ The mery moneth of September, / With the ix daye of the
same, / For then began our myrth and game." He invokes the
muse of tragedy, Melpomene,

> To guyde my pen and my pen to enbybe!
> Illumyn me, your poete and your scrybe,
> That with myxture of aloes and bytter gall
> I may compounde confectures for a cordiall,
> To angre the Scottes and Irysh keteringes withall.

He includes much of his earlier poem about the summoning:
"To you nothing it dyd accorde / To summon our kynge, your
soueraygne lord. / A kyng, a sumner! it was great wonder: /
Know ye not suger and salt asonder?"

This time he shows no doubt as to where the battle took place
and what were its results:

> Vnto the castell of Norram,
> I vnderstande, to sone ye came.
> At Branxston more and Flodden hylles,
> Our Englysh bowes, our Englysh bylles,
> Agaynst you gaue so sharpe a shower,
> That of Scotland ye lost the flower.

He credits Fortune with the victory: "Fortune on you therfore
did frowne; / Ye were to hye, ye are cast downe." And, to end
the poem, he batters and beats the "sumner": "Syr sumner, now
where is your crowne? / Cast of your crowne, cast vp your
crowne! / Syr sumner, now ye haue lost your crowne." This work
is signed, significantly enough, most flamboyantly: "Quod Skelton laureate, oratoure to the Kynges most royall estate."

As usual, however, there were some who complained of the
poet's bitter lines. And so, in a brief appendix "Vnto Diuers
People That Remord This Rymynge Agaynst the Scot Jemmy,"
he defended himself—"For some peoples sake / That lyst for to
iangyll / And waywardly to wrangyll / Agaynst this my makynge"
—by stating that James was a traitor to England and therefore
deserved such treatment. Worst of all, he saw the dead James
as a defector from Mother Church:

> He was a recrayed [recreant, false] knyght,
> A subtyll sysmatyke,
> Ryght nere an heretyke,
> Of grace out of the state,
> And died excomunycate.

This epilogue ends with a forthright question: *"Si veritatem dico,
quare non creditis mihi?"* (If I am telling the truth, why do you
not believe me?)

A brief but powerful *sarcasmos* (first in Latin and then in
English) against one particular Scot may date from a later time
—the outburst *Against Dundas*.[76] Here the *nobilis poeta*, as Skelton signs himself, seems more personal than national, ranting
against "This Dundas, / This Scottishe as, / He rymes and railes
/ That Englishmen haue tailes." The poet rushes in—

> Skelton laureat
> After this rate

> Defendeth with his pen
> All Englysh men
> Agayn Dundas,
> That Scottishe asse—

and piles up epithets in clipped alliterations: "Dundas, dronken and drowsy, / Skabed, scuruy, and lowsy, / Of vnhappy generacion / And most vngracious nacion." At the end, Skelton simply writes off Dundas with a warning: "Walke, Scot, / Walke, sot, / Rayle not to far."

b A FLYTING

Skelton was not quite done with Scotland, however, for the impulse for his *Poems Against Garnesche*[77] came from that country. These four tirades, composed in 1514, constitute one side of a "flyting"—the first that we know of in England, in fact—a literary contest in the hurling of insults. Much cultivated in Italy, this type of invective was well established in Scotland, where the famous *Flyting of Dunbar and Kennedy* took place around 1495 and was published in 1508.[78] Skelton's poems were modeled upon the Scottish exemplar and bear many similarities to Dunbar's. Skelton may even have known William Dunbar personally, for the great Scottish poet visited England several times. He was in London, for instance, from October, 1501, until January, 1502, when Skelton was employed at court; and Dunbar actually received a large gratuity from the King at this time.[79]

In the contest with the royal orator, ordered specifically "By the kynges most noble commandement," as Skelton carefully notes at the end of each section of the flyting, the Gentleman-Usher, Christopher Garnesche, was the challenger: "Sithe ye haue me chalyngyd, M[aster] Garnesche, / Ruduly revilyng me in the kynges noble hall. . . ." Unfortunately, none of Sir Christopher's literary efforts have survived; and we can only surmise what insults were laid upon the poet laureate.

The first of Skelton's four diatribes consists of six stanzas in stately rhyme royal, possibly judged most proper for court entertainment. The first three dwell on the fact that Garnesche has called Skelton a knave; the last three emphasize his more repulsive physical aspects. All stanzas have a similar refrain—"But sey me now, Syr Satrapas, what autoryte ye haue / In your chal-

enge, Syr Chystyn, to cale me knaue?—" except the last, when
Skelton throws the challenge right back at his adversary: "Boldly
bend you to batell, and buske [prepare] your selfe to saue: /
Chalenge your selfe for a fole, call me no more knaue." One
knight after another marches through these lines, as Skelton compares Garnesche to all manner of heroes from "Syr Tyrmagant"
to "Syr Topyas." Behind this comparison was undoubtedly the
fact that Garnesche was knighted in 1513 (on which basis the
flyting is now dated 1514).

Skelton's second blast tells us that Garnesche has called in
someone to second him in his literary duel—someone whom Skelton mocked as "greasy, Gorbellied Godfrey." [80] In form, this
poem matches the first—six stanzas of rhyme royal with a two-
line refrain. But in it much of the invective is aimed at Fat Godfrey: "How may I your mokery mekely tollerate, / [Your] gron-
ynge, zour grontynge, your groinyne lyke a swyne?" At the end,
Skelton merrily yokes Godfrey and his patron together—"Gup,
gorbellyd Godfrey, gup, Garnysche, gaudy fole! / To turney or to
tante with me ye ar to fare to seke"—and adds a favorite threat,
an echo of the *Miroir des Dames* in which one sees death:
"*Mirres vous y*, / Loke nat to hy." [81]

In the second half of the *flyting* (parts three and four), Skelton reverts to couplets for his invective, and he twits Garnesche
at great length about his youth in the home of Lady Brewes
(actually Christopher had been a page in the neighborhood great
house, according to the custom of the time), beginning,

> Whan ye war yonger of age,
> Ye war a kechyn page,
> A dyshwasher, a dryvyll,
> In the pott your nose dedde sneuyll;
> Ye fryed and ye broylyd,
> Ye rostyd and ye boylyd. . . .

In a cascade of endless couplets, Garnesche is again vilified
physically.

By the time Skelton finished his last tirade, he was in splendid
form, having been incited to battle by his opponent's latest rejoinder: "Garnyshe, gargone, gastly, gryme, / I haue receyuyd
your secunde ryme." He rants against his unskilled adversary,

who, although he knows his musical values (like the Comely
Coistrown—"Thowthe ye kan skylle of large and longe"), knows
nothing of verse writing and golden-tongued Cicero's *Rhetoric*.
Garnesche has in this "second rhyme" poked fun at Skelton's ancestry—and in reply to this, the laureate gives us some of the
most informative biographical bits about himself that we possess:

> A kyng to me myn habyte gaue:
> At Oxforth, the vniversyte,
> Auaunsid I was to that degre;
> By hole consent of theyr senate,
> I was made poete lawreate.

Here, too, are the lines telling of his tutoring young Henry ("The
honor of Englond I lernyd to spelle") and of "Aqueintyng hym
with the Musys nyne." The royal orator strikes back vigorously
at Garnesche, who surely has never reached such heights as this:

> Yt commyth thé wele me to remorde [find fault with],
> That creaunser [tutor] was to thy sofre[yne] lorde:
> It plesyth that noble prince roialle
> Me as hys master for to calle
> In hys learnyng primordialle.

Again, he warns the jolly rutterkin of his "inordynate pride":
"Presumptuous pride ys all thyn hope: / God garde thé, Gar-
nyche, from the rope!" And he protests once more at the end
that he is continuing the contest at the King's express pleasure:

> My study myght be better spynt;
> But for to serue the kynges entent,
> Hys noble pleasure and commandemennt,
> Scrybbyl thow, scrybyll thow, rayle or wryght,
> Wryght what thow wylte, I xall thé aquyte.

No records remain to tell us the outcome of the struggle. But
there can be little doubt, it would seem, as to who was adjudged
the more talented vilifier.

C MAGNIFICENCE

Skelton's entertainment for the court was not limited, however,
to flyting. He also tried his hand at the interlude, a new dramatic

form developing from and replacing the old morality play. *Magnificence* is the only one of his dramas that has survived, although he apparently wrote several others. In the *Garland of Laurel* he speaks "Of Vertu also the souerayne enterlude" and mentions "His commedy, Achademios callyd by name"; but he describes in detail the "notable mater" of *Magnyfycence,* calling by name its most memorable characters and giving the moral:

> And of Magnyfycence a notable mater,
> How Cownterfet Cowntenaunce of the new get
> With Crafty Conueyaunce dothe smater and flater,
> And Cloked Collucyoun is brought in to clater
> With Courtely Abusyoun; who pryntith it wele in mynde
> Moche dowblenes of the worlde therin he may fynde.[82]

Achademios may have been a Latin comedy written for performance at his Oxford laureation; and a play glorifying virtue— the royal characteristic *par excellence,* emphasized in the *Speculum principis*—would have been quite within the tradition. But no record of these plays exists. Thomas Warton, in his monumental *History of English Poetry,* describes another lost play of Skelton's—the *Necromancer,* which Warton says was printed by Wynken de Worde in 1504.[83]

In comparison with the older moralities, the play *Magnificence*[84] is significant for several reasons. Although the theme of the play is the old morality theme of virtues *versus* vices, the struggle is between prudence and folly rather than good and evil. Moreover, the aim of the virtues in the play is not to achieve salvation of the soul but worldly prosperity. The play, consequently, is filled with advice for living successfully in this world, rather than looking toward the next. The transition from religious to secular drama is seen, too, in the characters. For although Skelton draws upon the old abstractions (Good Hope, Redress, Perseverance on the one hand; Despair, Mischief on the other), he also introduces new types representing abuses at court: Counterfeit Countenance, Crafty Conveyance, Cloaked Collusion, and Courtly Abusion.

Magnificence, then, is political allegory, the first play to satirize the follies of court, especially lavish expenditure.[85] The ruler Magnificence, the only neutral character in the play, is first seen with his two attendants Wealth (Felicity) and Liberty; later, these are exchanged for Adversity and Poverty, after the four rogues representing court abuses have got the monarch well in hand. The political application is seen in the two rival parties fighting for power at Henry's court: the old aristocracy led by the Duke of Norfolk (represented by the five virtues in the play —Measure and Circumspection, in addition to those named above) and the newer powers dominated by Wolsey (represented by all the evil elements in the play). In fact, the six vices personify for the laureate Wolsey's own characteristics—the same qualities Skelton was to attack even more unmistakably in his later satires against the Cardinal. Some of these characters had already appeared in the *Bouge of Court*, which has many resemblances to *Magnificence*. Others are added (like Counterfeit Countenance, an obvious jibe at Wolsey's low origin) or transformed (like the ragged and tattered Riot in the *Bouge of Court*, who becomes Courtly Abusion, splendid in his extravagant dress) with Wolsey in mind.

Magnificence has long been dated 1516, largely on the basis of two references in it to "Kynge Lewes of Fraunce" (Louis XII, d. 1515), noted for his lavish spending: "For, syth he dyed, largesse was lytell vsed." There are no signs of act or scene divisions in the play, but, as Ramsay shows, the play falls naturally into five "stages," each having its own topic: Prosperity, Conspiracy, Delusion, Overthrow, and Restoration.[86] The first stage shows Magnificence with Felicity (Wealth), Liberty, and Measure, who states the theme in terms no one could miss:

> Where measure is mayster, plenty dothe none offence;
> Where measure lackyth, all thynge dysorderyd is;
> Where measure is absent, ryot kepeth resydence;
> Where measure is ruler, there is nothynge amysse;
> Measure is treasure. . . .

Even Liberty admits that Measure is right: "There is no prynce but he hath nede of vs thre, / Welthe, with Measure and pleasaunt Lyberte." Toward the end, one of the court fools, Fancy or Largesse, brings Magnificence a letter alleged to be from an absent advisor, Sad Circumspection, just as Counterfeit Countenance appears on the scene.

In contrast to this section with its prudent characters, the second stage (Conspiracy) shows the caperings and conversation of the other three gallants, Crafty Conveyance, Cloaked Collusion, and Courtly Abusion, each introduced under a false (and "good") name. Their aim, of course, is to control the prince. The second type of court fool, Folly, now enters—"*Hic ingrediatur* Foly, *quatiendo crema et faciendo multum, feriendo tabulas et similia*" (Enter Folly, shaking his bauble and capering about, playing on instruments and the like)—and joins with Fancy in a marvelous nonsensical duet composed of rushing, tumbling lines.

The third act (Delusion) shows the prince consorting freely with the four charming gallants and completely in their hands. In a magnificent speech, truly worthy of a king, he displays his royal *hybris* to the extent that he has no fear even of Fortune:

> Fortune to her lawys can not abandune me,
> But I shall of Fortune rule the reyne;
> I fere nothynge Fortunes perplexyte;
> All honour to me must nedys stowpe and lene.

The prince promises Courtly Abusion to spend thousands on pleasures, and Measure is banished altogether. At the end, however, Magnificence begins to see how he has been cheated of all his wealth—"vndone with stelyng and robbynge," as grim Adversity enters.

The last two stages of the play (Overthrow and Restoration), more religious than political, follow the pattern of the traditional morality play. Magnificence, now "*beten downe, and spoylyd from all his goodys and rayment*," is thoroughly dressed down by Adversity, who begins, "The stroke of God, Aduersyte I hyght; / I pluke downe kynge, prynce, Lorde, and knyght"; and then he gives a most realistic account of the ills in the world. After this, Poverty takes over, and the prince bewails his fate: "Alasse, where is nowe my golde and fe? / Alasse, I say, where to am I brought? / Alasse, alasse, alasse, I dye for thought!"

The evil counselors laugh and jape at the deluded prince, leaving him quite ripe for Despair, who assures Magnificence that there is no hope for him on earth or in heaven. Mischief provides a knife, and the prince is ready to use it when he is rescued by Goodhope. Redress, Sad Circumspection, and Perseverance all have a part in the Restoration; and Magnificence rises a sadder and wiser prince. Sad Circumspection pronounces the moral, in case anyone has missed it:

> A myrrour incleryd is this interlude,
> This lyfe inconstant for to beholde and se;
> Sodenly auaunsyd, and sodenly subdude,
> Sodenly ryches, and sodenly pouerte,
> Sodenly comfort, and sodenly aduersyte;
> Sodenly thus Fortune can bothe smyle and frowne,
> Sodenly set vp, and sodenly cast downe.

The last two lines, in fact, form a refrain in Circumspection's two-stanza (rhyme-royal) monologue. Perseverance underlines the moral, beginning, "This treatyse, deuysyd to make you dysporte, / Sheweth nowe adayes howe the worlde comberyd is," and ending, "To day a man, to morowe he lyeth in the duste; / Thus in this worlde there is no erthly truste." Magnificence shows that he has learned his lesson: "This mater we haue mouyd, you myrthys to make, . . . / Thus none estate lyuynge of hym can be sure, / For the welthe of this worlde can not indure." And Redress pronounces the benediction for the audience: "And ye that haue harde this dysporte and game, / Jhesus preserue you frome endlesse wo and shame! / Amen."

Although a brief synopsis of the play sounds solemn and heavy, *Magnificence* is in fact lightened by a good deal of mirth, sport, and play. Fancy and Folly—one the "natural," the other the "artificial" fool [87]—have endless opportunities to amuse the audience, as do the four court gallants, with their affectations and dancing steps. Folly's picking a non-existent louse from the shoulder of Crafty Conveyance is a jape worthy of Patch himself. Courtly Abusion has all the earmarks of the comic Flemish upstart, the "jolly rutterkin," as he enters singing bits of "Roti bouilli joyeulx" and other dance tunes.[88] The nonsense duet in antiphonal verse between the two fools has no other aim than to amuse (although there undoubtedly are topical allusions that would point up the humor to an audience of 1516), as one fool gives a line and the other completes the couplet:

> *Fan.* Nowe thou hast done me a pleasure grete.
> *Fol.* In faythe, I wolde thou had a marmosete.
> *Fan.* Cockes harte, I loue suche iapes.
> *Fol.* Ye for all thy mynde is on owles and apes.

And when Folly performs alone, the resulting gibberish makes admirable fooling indeed:

> Sym Sadylgose was my syre, and Dawcocke my dame:
> I coude, and I lyst, garre [make] you laughe at a game,
> Howe a wodcocke wrastled with a larke that was lame:
> The bytter sayd boldly that they were to blame;
> The feldfare wolde haue fydled, and it wolde not frame [succeed];
> The crane and the curlewe therat gan to grame;
> The snyte snyueled in the snowte and smyled at the game.

Even Magnificence is astounded at this virtuosity: "Cockes bones, herde you euer suche another?" And at least once, in the depth of his misery, the prince himself must have had the royal on-lookers in gales of laughter, as he *dolorously maketh his mone,* mocking the traditional rhetoric of the lament:

> O feble fortune, O doulfull destyny!
> O hatefull happe, O carefull cruelte!
> O syghynge sorowe, O thoughtfull mysere!
> O rydlesse rewthe, O paynfull pouerte!
> O dolorous herte, O harde aduersyte!
> O odyous dystresse, O dedly payne and woo!
> For worldly shame I was bothe wanne and bloo [livid].

Frequent changes in verse forms[89] also make for lightness of touch and, at the same time, point up characterization. Magnificence, of course, invariably speaks in the stately rhyme-royal pattern, as do the wise old counselors, Sad Circumspection, Redress, Perseverance. The court gallants are limited to no one type. Courtly Abusion, however, the most musically gifted of them all, is uniquely set apart by a lyric in exquisitely brief lines, detailing preciously the new French fashions (the "new jet") he has brought to court:

> My heyre bussheth [brusheth]
> So pleasuntly,

My robe russheth
So ruttyngly,
Me seme I flye,
I am so lyght,
To daunce delyght;
Properly drest,
All poynte deuyse,
My persone prest
Beyonde all syse
Of the newe gyse. . . .

And the fools shift easily back and forth, singly or together, from long to short lines, from couplets to quatrains, from traditional rhetoric to alliterative Skeltonics. Fancy runs the gamut in one speech as freely as a well-trained soprano sliding easily from head to chest tones:

Lo, this is
My fansy, I wys.
. . . .
Somtyme to sober, somtyme to sadde,
Sometyme to mery, somtyme to madde,
Somtyme I syt as I were solempe prowde;
Somtyme I laughe ouer lowde.

. . . .
I blunder, I bluster, I blowe, and I blother;
I make on the one day, and I marre on the other;
Bysy, bysy, and euer bysy,
I daunce vp and downe tyll I am dyssy.

Magnificence is, then, a mixture of old and new, of seriousness and humor, of traditional religion and practical politics. Its hero is Henry VIII and at the same time any man whom adverse Fortune may cast down at any time.[90] Its vices add up to Thomas Wolsey, or to anyone else motivated by extreme self-love and selfish ambition. Its virtue *par excellence* is moderation, to describe which, Skelton finds musical terminology (completely comprehensible to his aristocratic audience) most effective. Measure himself says, "All trebyllys and tenours be rulyd by a meyne," referring to the voice between treble and tenor. Later, Magnificence explains, in musical terms altogether:

Measure and I wyll neuer be deuydyd
For no dyscorde that any man can sawe;
For measure is a meane, nother to hy nor to lawe,
In whose attemperaunce I haue suche delyght,
That measure shall neuer departe from my syght.[91]

Just before his downfall, however, Magnificence defies Fortune
—"Fortune to her lawys can not abandune me, / But I shall of
Fortune rule the reyne"—and boasts of having abandoned Measure in the same musical terms: "I synge of two partys without
a mene." Skelton is consistent, too, in describing Fortune as leading a dance (as in his earlier works). Poverty, for instance, reminds Magnificence: "Syr, remember the tourne of Fortunes
whele, / That wantonly can wynke, and wynche with her hele.
. . . / She dawnsyth varyaunce with mutabylyte."

d AGAINST VENOMOUS TONGUES

Overtones of Magnificence are heard in a short, sharp indict-
ment Against Venomous Tongues,[92] when the poet warns, "Such
tunges vnhappy hath made great diuision / In realmes, in cities,
by suche fals abusion; / Of fals fickil tunges suche cloked collusion / Hath brought nobil princes to extreme confusion." This
rejoinder was the result, apparently, of slander against the royal
orator for trying to wield too much influence at court: "Who
soeuer that tale vnto you tolde, / He saith vntruly, to say that I
would / Controlle the cognisaunce of noble men / Either by
language or with my pen." Skelton claims he is above all such:
"My scole is more solem and somwhat more haute / Than to be
founde in any such faute." The owner of the "false, lying tongue"
was obviously unknown to the poet, who can only threaten: "But
if that I knewe what his name hight, / For clatering of me I
would him sone quight; / For his false lying, of that I spake
neuer, / I could make him shortly repent him for euer."

The poem begins in couplets, but as the poet's rage mounts,
so do the rhymes—often to four, twice to seven. As to the "occasion" for this tirade—"For ye said, that he said, that I said, wote
ye what?"—and the real "matter" of it, opinions differ. It has long
been thought that the poem resulted from the general hostility
aroused by the performance at court of Magnificence. But recent
scholarship leads one to think that it may have been written be-

fore the interlude, and that Skelton refers to *Magnificence* at the
end of his poem when he adds the Latin gloss that he intends to
write a work "holy, praiseworthy, acceptable, memorable, and
honorable":

> Wherof hereafter I thinke for to write,
> Of fals double tunges in the dispite.
> *Recipit se scripturum opus sanctum, laudabile, acceptabile,*
> *memorabileque, et nimis honorificandum.*

Edwards has worked out the meaning behind the curious
verses, "For before on your brest, and behind on your back, /
In Romaine letters I neuer founde lack," and the Latin gloss referring to Roman letters on the liveries of followers.[93] One of
Wolsey's followers (who wore the letters "TC" embroidered on
the backs and breasts of their coats) complained to Wolsey of
Skelton's critical remarks (a jibe, perhaps, at "more letters than
learning"?) about all the ostentatious display when Thomas was
invested Cardinal (September 10, 1515) and at other times. And
Pollet has connected all this with the so-called "interview at Tottenham" (May 4, 1516), actually mentioned in Skelton's poem:
"What tidings at Totnam, what newis in Wales?"[94] At this meeting with Henry VIII and his sister Margaret of Scotland, Wolsey
managed to push through a policy limiting the number of retainers in livery that any nobleman could keep, a policy much
opposed, naturally, by the old aristocracy. Skelton, then, had
been accused by someone of siding with the old nobility, some
of whom—including his own patron, the Earl of Northumberland—had been committed to Fleet Prison for keeping too many
retainers.

In speaking out for the conservative party against Wolsey, with
his tremendous display of liveried followers, the royal orator
would inevitably have invited the Cardinal's wrath. And this
situation seems to be what brought on the tirade against false,
lying tongues—the first poem, as far as we know, aimed directly
at Lord Thomas. Similarities between the poem and *Magnificence*, thus, appear to be foreshadowings rather than echoes.

e SPEAK, PARROT

There are quite definite echoes of *Magnificence* in what is now
regarded as Skelton's masterpiece written, probably, in 1521:

Speke, Parrot.[95] Fancy's lines in the interlude, "Bysy, bysy, and euer bysy, / I daunce vp and downe tyll I am dyssy," are recalled to us in a stanza near the beginning of *Speak, Parrot* that characterizes the entire poem:

> Besy, besy, besy, and besynes agayne!
>> *Que pensez voz,* Parrot? what meneth this besynes?
> *Vitulus* in Oreb troubled Arons brayne,
>> Melchisedeck mercyfull made Moloc mercyles;
>> To wyse is no vertue, to medlyng, to restles;
> In mesure is tresure, *cum sensu maturato;*
> *Ne tropo sanno, ne tropo mato.*

The jibe at Wolsey's busy meddling, comparison with useless Old Testament activities, the mingling of languages, the pounding home of the moral—all these are found over and over in this most elusive of all Skelton's poems. Parrot, in fact, is to speak his piece under the cloak of allegory and metaphor:

> But of that supposicyon that callyd is arte
>> *Confuse distributive,* as Parrot hath deuysed,
> Let euery man after his merit take his parte,
>> For in this processe Parrot nothing hath surmysed,
>> No matter pretendyd, nor nothyng enterprysed,
> But that *metaphora, allegoria* with all,
> Shall be his protectyon, his pauys, and his wall.

A large part of the metaphor that helps to make this *"Confuse distributive"* (methodical confusion) has to do, of course, with Parrot himself. Who is Parrot? "Parot is my owne dere harte and my dere derling," his beak burnished by Melpomene, the Muse of tragedy; "Parrot is a fayre byrd for a lady, . . . / Make moche of Parrot, the popegay ryall." As one reads the poem, it becomes abundantly clear that the "royal popinjay" is undoubtedly Skelton himself, in his role of *vates*—bard, prophet, and seer. Much of the long first part of the poem (composed of many sections, written at various times) refers directly to Skelton.

The opening stanzas of the poem find the "byrd of paradyse" [96] daintily and richly living among "great ladyes of estate":

> My name is Parrot, a byrd of paradyse,
>> By nature deuysed of a wonderous kynde,

    Dyentely dyeted with dyuers dylycate spyce,
     Tyl Euphrates, that flode, dryueth me into Inde;
     Where men of that countrey by fortune me fynd,
    And send me to greate ladyes of estate;
    Then Parot must haue an almon or a date;

    A cage curyously caruen, with syluer pyn,
     Properly paynted, to be my couertowre;
    A myrrour of glasse, that I may toote [peep] therin;
     These maidens ful mekely with many a diuers flowre
     Freshly they dresse, and make swete my bowre,
    With, Speke, Parrot, I pray you, full curtesly they say;
    Parrot is a goodly byrd, a prety popagey.

Parrot knows bits of many languages: French and the five languages of the new humanism, just coming in—Hebrew, Arabic, Chaldaic, in addition to Latin and Greek. He is completely loyal to the King and Queen: "Cryst saue Kyng Henry the viii., our royall kyng, / The red rose in honour to florysh and sprynge! / With Kateryne incomparable, our ryall quene also, / That pereles pomegarnet, Chryst saue her noble grace!" He has served dame Philology: "My lady maystres, dame Philology, / Gaue me a gyfte in my nest whan I laye, / To lerne all language, and it to spake aptely"—but he has sometimes spoken out too freely, although he knows that "Dyscressyon is moder of noble vertues all," and he must be more careful: "*Hæc res acu tangitur,* Parrot, *par ma foy: / Ticez vous,* Parrot, *tenez vous coye.*"

But Parrot is anxious to speak: "I pray you, let Parot haue lyberte to speke." He is happily situated "amonge ladyes" delighting in "solas, pleasure, dysporte, and pley"; but he is not unaware of danger: "But ware the cat, Parot, ware the fals cat!" He knows how to please the King ("Parot can say, *Cæsar, aue,* also") although he is no longer in favor at court ("But Parrot hath no fauour to Esebon" [Heshbon, that is, London]). And so "Parrot pretendith to be a bybyll clarke" and bewails the evils of London life comparable to those of Old Testament times. He emphasizes the fact that the traitor Wolsey is far too powerful: "With, He sayd, and we said, ich wot now what ich wot, / *Quod magnus est dominus Judas Scarioth.*" Wolsey has even invaded academe, which has never been in such a sad state: "*In Academia* Parrot dare no probleme kepe; . . . / Tryuyals and quatryuyals

so sore now they appayre, / That Parrot the popagay hath pytye
to beholde / How the rest of good lernyng is roufled vp and
trold."

Parrot ends this first section with an idea never far from Skelton's thought—a reminder that all is vanity "Except mannes
soule, that Chryst so dere bought," and that "Pompe, pryde, honour, ryches, and worldly lust, / Parrot sayth playnly, shall tourne
all to dust." And so Parrot presents his little "recule" (collection)
to the ladies for whom he has written it: "Thus Parrot dothe
pray you / With hert most tender, / To rekyn with this recule
now, / And it to remember."

The rest of the poem is composed of bits and pieces, such as
might be copied out in a commonplace book—poetry, prose,
English, French, Latin, religion, science, riddles, and proverbs.[97]
There is a ballad, "My propire Besse," which has never been
satisfactorily explained.[98] Elizabeth of York, wife of Henry VII,
was known affectionately as Lady Bessy; and the inclusion of the
ballad may be Skelton's way of proclaiming once again his loyalty to the Yorkists and their connections—the old conservative
aristocracy. There is a tiny quatrain that looks like the beginning
of an "ABC" poem,[99] aimed, obviously, at the Cardinal: "Amen,
Amen, / And set to a D, / And then it is, Amend / Our new
found A, B, C."

And then there are four envoys, in which the barbs against
Wolsey become plainer and stronger. The first three of these
refer to the Cardinal's ostentatious but ineffectual mission to
Calais, 1521, to act as mediator between Francis I and Charles
V; the message of the poems is that Wolsey stop wasting time
and money and come home[100]—as in the *Secunde Lenuoy* (where
he is compared to Zadok the high priest):

> Passe forthe, Parotte, towardes some passengere,
>   Require hym to convey yow ovyr the salte fome;
> Addressyng your selfe, lyke a sadde messengere,
>   To ower soleyne seigneour Sadoke, desire hym to cum
>   home. . . .

A short dialogue between Galathea and Parrot follows, in
which Galathea keeps urging the bird to speak: "Speke, Parotte,
my swete byrde, and ye shall haue a date, / Of frantycknes and

folysshnes whyche ys the grett state?" The "royal popinjay" does indeed speak out against the Cardinal in terms now unmistakable:

> Frantiknes dothe rule and all thyng commaunde;
> Wylfulnes and braynles no[w] rule all the raye;
> Agayne ffrentike frenesy there dar no man sey nay,
> For ffrantiknes, and wylfulnes, and braynles ensembyll,
> The nebbis of a lyon they make to trete and trembyll.

Punning on cards and card-games, the speaker clearly identifies the prelate: "He caryeth a kyng in hys sleve, yf all the worlde fayle; / He facithe owte at a fflusshe, with, shewe, take all! / Of Pope Julius cardys he ys chefe cardynall." With a pun on "wolf's head," Parrot pounds away at the Cardinal's influence over the King:

> He tryhumfythe, he trumpythe, he turnythe all vp and downe,
> With, skyregalyard, prowde palyard, vaunteperler, ye prate!
> Hys woluys hede, wanne, bloo as lede, gapythe over the crowne:
> Hyt ys to fere leste he wolde were the garland on hys pate.

Parrot now asks for his reward: "Now, Galathea, lett Parrot, I pray yow, haue hys date." But the lady is not satisfied: "Nowe, Parott, my swete byrde, speke owte yet ons agayne, / Sette asyde all sophysms, and speke now trew and playne."

And so Parrot goes into one of his "so much this, so little that" outbursts (reminiscent of his earlier poem *The Maner of the World Now a Dayes*), with a varying refrain, beginning, "Syns Dewcalyons flodde. . . ." [101] The entire poem, in fact, comes to a great climax at this point with reference to the butcher's son (much was made of Wolsey's low origin during his lifetime), the Tudor greyhound, and the Buckingham swan:

> So braynles caluys hedes, so many shepis taylys;
> So bolde a braggyng bocher, and flesshe sold so dere;
> So many plucte partryches, and so fatte quaylles;
> So mangye a mastyfe curre, the grete grey houndes pere:
> So bygge a bulke of brow auntlers cabagyd that yere;
> So many swannes dede, and so small revell;—
> Syns Dewcalyons flodde, I trow, no man can tell.

From politics, Parrot turns to evils in the church—"So myche decay of monesteries and of relygious places; / So hote hatered agaynste the Chyrche, and cheryte so colde"—and finally to the Cardinal's more loathesome personality and habits: "So rygorous revelyng in a prelate specially; / So bold and so braggyng, and was so baselye borne; . . . / So fatte a magott, bred of flesshe flye; / Was nevyr suche ffylty gorgon, nor suche an epycure. . . ." Parrot ends his speech in a pontifical manner: "*Dixit*, quod Parrot." And the laureate cannot refrain from adding a Latin epigram to the effect that "This Parrot will grow immensely during my lifetime; hence my glorious Skeltonic fame will be celebrated."

Who are the ladies of great estate who have received Parrot so kindly and who keep urging him to speak? Galathea is probably meant to be Elizabeth, Countess of Surrey: this identification makes more meaningful the inclusion of the little song to Besse.[102] Moreover, Elizabeth was the daughter of the Duke of Buckingham, who was beheaded for no other reason than that he opposed Wolsey's policies.[103] Second wife of Thomas Howard, Earl of Surrey (and later Duke of Norfolk), Elizabeth was just the person to keep urging Parrot to speak out against the murderer of her father and the enemy of her husband. Sometime during 1521, then, Skelton had apparently abandoned—temporarily, at least—the Royal Court in London for the more tranquil surroundings of the Howard family in one of their country homes (possibly Sheriff-Hutton in Yorkshire).

Thus the poem that at first reading seems an unintelligible jumble, a collection of "studied gibberish," turns out to be informed throughout by one basic idea. John Holloway has well summed up the matter.[104] "Everything which shows Skelton's place in the culture of his time," he writes,

seems to converge in this poem. Morality based upon the Bible and the people's proverbial wisdom goes here with an essentially vernacular use of language throughout, with a distinctive development of the polyglot macaronic kind of writing (a popular and goliardic mode rather than a literary one), and with a structure perhaps, somewhat like those commonplace books which passed from hand to hand in the country houses of the time. . . . Yet out of this gallimaufry, Skelton has made a poem which (though a chaos from a mechanical standpoint) is imaginatively perhaps the most unified of his works. It is unified in the persistent vivid presence and exceedingly distinctive tone—the tone of one who threatens and is himself in danger—of the parrot itself. Above all it is unified in the gathering power and directness of the attack as this gradually breaks through the speaker's prudence, and at last converts his glancing blows into the finale: a fierce and solemn denuciation of Wolsey himself. . . . The passionate, unflinching, comprehensive grasp of reality, and embodiment of it in an idiom wholly the writer's own, are unmistakable. If we think that we are not in the presence here of poetic greatness, it is because there is a kind of poetic greatness which we have not learnt to know.

f COLIN CLOUT

Although *Speak, Parrot* with its myriads of esoteric references was geared to a small and knowledgeable audience, Skelton's next attack on the Cardinal was of a different sort altogether: the message of *Colyn Cloute*[105] was plain for all to see. Here the poet appears in the guise of a simple man of the people, who reports what he hears among layfolk of ecclesiastical evils: "Thus I, Colyn Cloute, / As I go aboute, / And wandrynge as I walke, / I here the people talke." But Colin makes it abundantly clear that he speaks only against wicked priests and prelates; only if the shoe fits, he says, should one wear it:

> Of no good bysshop speke I,
> Nor good preest I escrye,
> Good frere, nor good chanon,
> Good nonne, nor good canon,
> Good monke, nor good clercke,
> Nor yette of no good werke:
> But my recountyng is
> Of them that do amys,
> In speking and rebellyng,
> In hynderyng and dysauaylyng
> Holy Churche, our mother,
> One agaynst another.

The entire poem is one great, unified, perpendicular structure of 1270 lines. Typical of Skelton's strong sense of propriety in characterization, the verse form is not the stately rhyme royal of *Magnificence* and *Speak, Parrot*: it is the simple Skeltonic half-line of two beats, a line that never changes throughout the poem, in rhymes of two or more. Colin himself protests that he is no poet of the laureate tradition, that what he has to say is what is important:

> For though my ryme be ragged,
> Tattered and iagged,
> Rudely rayne beaten,
> Rusty and moughte eaten,
> If ye take well therwith,
> It hath in it some pyth.

Read closely, however, *Colin Clout* seems to fall naturally into two parts, differing not in kind but in intensity.

The first section (lines 1–488) begins *in medias res* by railing against the futility of trying to reach someone whose "hed is so fat,"

> He wotteth neuer what
> Nor wherof he speketh;
> He cryeth and he creketh,
> He pryeth and he peketh,
> He chydes and he chatters,
> He prates and he patters,
> He clytters and he clatters,
> He medles and he smatters,
> He gloses and he flatters;
>
> . . . .
>
> He is but a fole;
> Let hym go to scole.

Many details follow about how the hungry sheep look up and are not fed—how "The remenaunt is amys / Of the clergy all, / Bothe great and small." But however far afield Colin gets in recounting the ills of the Church in general and of the greed, illiteracy, neglect, ambition, and riotous living on the part of the priesthood, the poet invariably keeps returning to one prelate in particular. The realistic description of the churchman riding upon a mule—"With golde all betrapped, / In purple and paule belapped"—is an obvious jibe at Wolsey, whose ostentation in procession was well known.[106] Invariably, too, the laureate returns to his favorite idea that "pride goeth before a fall"; and the first part of the poem ends with what has long been known as "Skelton's prophecy." [107] Astrology has foretold, he says,

A fatall fall of one
That shuld syt on a trone,
And rule all thynges alone.

. . . .

After *gloria, laus,*
May come a soure sauce;
Sory therfore am I,
But trouth can neuer lye.

It is here that a dynamic change is perceptible in what Colin
has to say. The laureate himself opens the second part of his
poem with a reference to this intensification in musical terms.
He intends to tune up his poetic harp, he says, and pitch his
accusations higher:

My penne nowe wyll I sharpe,
And wrest vp my harpe
With sharpe twynkyng trebelles,
Agaynst all suche rebelles
That laboure to confounde
And bryng the Churche to the grounde.

(There is even a musical pun on the word *ground,* of course,
meaning *bass* [*base*].) The intensity is seen in the larger issues
that are now the subject of satire—the encroachment of Lutheran and other heresies, the dissolution of certain monastic
establishments by Wolsey, the hypocrisy among the friars, the
over-lavish spending on the part of prelates, and the too great
influence of one "busy" man over the King. The "sharp, twinking
trebles" are seen, too, in the intensified rhetoric, as Colin warms
to his task: the increased use of *repetitio* and catalogues, the
piling of rhymes, the frequent occurrence of learned words, as
when

Some make epylogacyon
Of hyghe predestynacyon;
And of resydeuacyon
They make interpretacyon
Of an aquarde facyon.

But always one man is singled out for distinction—one man so
powerful that no one may even approach "our souerayne lorde"

> Without the assent
> Of our presydent,
>
> . . . .
>
> Nor to speke to hym secretly,
> Openly nor preuyly,
> Without his presydent be by,
> Or els his substytute
> Whom he wyll depute.

To illustrate gluttony and hypocrisy, Colin describes at great
length the luxurious tapestries in Wolsey's magnificent palace,
Hampton Court—"Hangynge aboute the walles / Clothes of
golde and palles"— depicting amorous scenes from Petrarch's
Triumphs:[108]

> Wyth dame Dyana naked;
> Howe lusty Venus quaked
>
> . . . .
>
> And howe Parys of Troy
> Daunced a lege de moy,
> Made lusty sporte and ioy
> With dame Helyn the quene. . . .

Regarding the old, conservative aristocracy, comments Colin,
"For the lordes temporall, / Theyr rule is very small, / Almost
nothyng at all." Colin reflects again, however, that although "It
is a besy thyng / For one man to rule a kyng . . . / Fortune
may chaunce to flyt / And whan he weneth to syt, / Yet may he
mysse the quysshon." As history richly demonstrated, this predic-
tion was an understatement of Wolsey's later comedown in the
world. Colin finally brings his report to an end: "Lo, this is the
gyse now a dayes!" he exclaims. Since he has not been able to
get "this boke" "By hoke ne by croke / Prynted for to be,"
it now seems best to lay down his pen, rest awhile, and lie at
anchor "Tyll the cost be clere"—probably a reference to his
safety from the Cardinal's wrath as long as he remains well pro-
tected. A brief Latin epilogue bemoans the decay of the once
honored laurel and the fact that the laureate is forbidden to
speak.

Critics are generally agreed that *Colin Clout* was written in
1522, by which time the laureate was back in the sanctuary of

Westminster. Actually, there is nothing in the poem to limit its place of composition to London. The date 1522 has been established by means of certain topical allusions in the poem (in addition to the fact that it is mentioned in the *Garland of Laurel,* printed in 1523). First, there is the reference to nuns being turned "Out of theyr cloyster and quere" and driven to prostitution, and also "Howe ye brake the dedes wylles, / Turne monasteris into water miles." Skelton appears to be commenting here on the fact that in 1521–22 two religious foundations (both for nuns) were dissolved, for the first time in more than a decade; one of these did indeed own a water mill.[109] And again, the lines (205–6) charging "some" churchmen with eating meat in Lent obviously refer to Wolsey's dispensations of 1522 for easing the rule against meat during the Lenten season.[110]

g ELINOR RUMMING

The most perennially popular of all Skelton's poems, *The Tunnyng of Elynour Rummynge,*[111] has never been satisfactorily dated. Its style, however, is quite similar to the style "now trew and playne" of *Colin Clout* with which Skelton associates it in the *Garland of Laurel.* The two-beat line is the same, and there is the same use of *repetitio* and alliteration, the piling-up of rhymes, the catalogues, the introduction of simple names (Margery, Maud). The laureate, then, may have turned momentarily in 1522 from his serious campaign against Wolsey to a lighter type of verse—a boisterous poem about an ale-wife and her grotesque customers.

The subject of the poem is the mistress of a tavern at Leatherhead, Surrey—the Running Horse, which is still partially standing:[112] "She dwelt in Sothray, / In a certayne stede / Bysyde Lederhede." In a way—some critics think a deliberate way—the poem complements the "Commendations" in *Philip Sparrow:* for Elinor's ugliness is described as meticulously as Jane's beauty. The poem opens, in fact, with a catalogue of Elinor's physical non-attractions based upon the rhetorical pattern of Geoffrey de Vinsauf. From her "lothely lere" (complexion) to her "shone smered wyth talowe" her outward appearance is carefully delineated: face, lips, nose, skin, eyes, hair, bones, feet, dress, and shoes.

The seven "fits" (cantos) that follow describe in galloping Skeltonics Elinor's "tunning" (brewing), her tavern, her habits,

and her clientele. Her ale is brewed according to a somewhat
unusual formula:

> The hennes donge away,
> And skommeth it into a tray
> Whereas the yeest is,
> With her maungy fystis:
> And somtyme she blennes
> The donge of her hennes
> And the ale together.

Her tavern is open to any livestock that may wander in: "The
sowe with her pygges; / The bore his tayle wrygges, / His rumpe
also he frygges / Agaynst the hye benche!" And her customers
are the dregs of local society: "A sorte of foule drabbes / All
scuruy with scabbes."

The poet—who may have actually sat in a corner of the Running Horse and witnessed "this mad mummynge" sometime when
the court was at Richmond in Surrey—presents a robust carica-
ture of the slatternly women who converge upon the ale-house
for their mid-morning draughts. Some he calls by name—"Kate,
Cysly, and Sare," "mad Kyt," and "Margery Mylkeducke." And
not only is the poet fascinated by this "solempne drinkynge": he
is intrigued also with the bartering. Articles exchanged for ale
would easily furnish a household:

> Some brought a wymble,
> Some brought a thymble,
> Some brought a sylke lace,
> Some brought a pyncase,
> Some her husbandes gowne,
> Some a pyllow of downe.

Animals, poultry, farm produce—all is grist for Elinor's mill:

> Another sorte of sluttes,
> Some brought walnuttes,
> Some apples, some peres,
> Some brought theyr clyppynge sheres,
> Some brought this and that,
> Some brought I wote nere what,
> Some brought theyr husbandes hat,

> Some podynges and lynkes,
> Some trypes that stynkes.

The poet hammers away, stopping only when he feels writer's cramp: "For my fyngers ytche; / I haue wrytten to mytche / Of this mad mummynge / Of Elynour Rummynge." But the laureate cannot refrain from adding at the end Latin lines inviting all drunken and sluttish women "to hear this little book."

These Latin verses, however, contain more than a hint of Skelton's attitude toward the poem: "*hæc loca plena jocis*," he says— these places are filled with jesting. He continues, as Rabelais deep in the "Querelle des Femmes" might have done, by telling us that his little book will sing a paean to drunken, squalid, sordid, talkative women, "sounding with their tongues the matter of laughter in a raucous song." [113] The poet, thus, took himself far less seriously here than many of his critics have done. Early critics saw a most immoral poem in *Elinor Rumming*. Pope's epithet "beastly," in fact, was probably aimed at the author of this poem, a copy of which was reprinted in 1718. [114] But even Skelton's admirers in the twentieth century continue to find in the poem "deadly satire", or at least "an underlying moral purpose." [115] Surely John Holloway is nearer the mark when he observes of this most misjudged of all Skelton's poems that its extraordinary vividness has prevented readers from grasping its full range. "It is not a moralizing poem," Holloway states, "but it is full of an awareness of the essential humanity of the scene it depicts." [116]

The idea of writing verses about the goings-on in an alehouse did not originate with Skelton, nor did *Elinor* emerge full-blown from the poet's imagination. Among antecedents, perhaps the best known are William Langland's description of Gluttony in the Ale-House (*Piers Plowman*, V) and Lydgate's *Ballade on an Ale-Seller*. Skelton's poem may owe something, too, to Dunbar's *Tydingis fra the Sessioun*, where there are long passages telling how "some do this, some do that." [117] Closest of all to *Elinor Rumming*, however, at least in bare outline, is a fifteenth-century song describing in many short stanzas a group of women drinking and gossiping in a tavern—women whose names are identical with Skelton's gossips: Elynore, Jone, Margery, Alis, Cecely. [118] Lacking the liveliness and vividness of Skelton's touch, this poem nonetheless may have given the laureate the idea of immortalizing the Leatherhead ale-wife in magnificent fits of verse. Finally, Skelton's poem may have owed some of its inspiration to the laureate's own acquaintance with a famous ale-seller in Westminster: Long Meg. At any event, *The Life of Long Meg of Westminster,* published in 1635 but said to have had a much earlier edition, contains a story in which "sir James of Castile, doctor Skelton, and Will Sommers" all participate, obviously very much at home at the Eagle Tavern.[119]

But whatever its ancestry in moral verse or balladry, *Elinor Rumming* is surely the poet's masterpiece among his works exploiting the short-line Skeltonic. And lest anyone view the poem as the work of a moment, the laureate himself tells us that to make successful "trifles" requires cunning, as he refers to *Elinor* and kindred pieces in the *Garland of Laurel:*

> Also the Tunnynge of Elinour Rummyng,
>   With Colyn Clowt, Iohnn Iue, with Ioforth Iack;
> To make suche trifels it asketh sum konnyng,
>   In honest myrth parde requyreth no lack;
>   The whyte apperyth the better for the black.[120]

If the black is all too plain in *Elinor,* the white is there too, if one looks for it—in the peaceful, quiet women who come for ale; in the sense of decorum, rough, to be sure, but genuine; in Elinor's handling of her customers; and in Elinor herself. Fearless, hard-working Elinor, as business woman and as literary character, has *endured:* here is another side to the opening couplets on Elinor, and to the descriptions of some of her friends. Finally, sheer joy in all the *things* of this world pervades the poem. There is no slightest sign here of *memento mori,* of returning to dust. *Elinor Rumming* is, in fact, the perfect example of the other side of the coin; it is the perfect antithesis to the all-flesh-is-grass theme seldom absent from the mind of the laureate.

Little wonder, then, that the poem was printed often and that even after Skelton's death, echoes of *Elinor* resounded in his parish. It is significant of the poem's great popularity that the Keeper of the Manors, Westminster, scribbled on the margin of his account book (1530–33), in order to test his pen: "Dame Elyner of Rumyng by her mumyng dumeryng." [121]

h WHY COME YE NOT TO COURT?

Most outspoken of all was Skelton's last attack on the Cardinal: *Why Come Ye Nat to Courte?* [122] In certain respects it forms a companion piece to *Colin Clout,* in which Wolsey was made the focus for all the ecclesiastical ills in the land; but the later poem attacks the Cardinal as a political figure. There is here, however, none of the great monolithic design of *Colin Clout.* This "lytell boke . . . compyled" by the laureate is obviously a collection of many short pieces similar to the ballads that represented journalism in his day and were written at white heat at the actual time of the occurrences commented upon. Nor is the poet's persona that of Colin, the simple layman: he is now the assured spokesman of the old aristocracy, who bitterly opposed Wolsey's policies with regard to the war against France. The poet's Latin motto, which he has placed at beginning and end of the poem, makes this abundantly clear: *"Hæc vates ille / De quo loquuntur mille"* ("Thus the bard wrote / Whom millions quote," as Edwards translates it [123]). Near the end of the poem, Skelton refers again to its wide audience:

> Some men myght aske a question,
> By whose suggestyon
> I toke on hand this warke,
> Thus boldly for to barke?
> And men lyst to harke,
> And my wordes marke,
> I wyll answere lyke a clerke.

And he answers by naming and quoting Juvenal to the effect that it is difficult not to write satire:

> I am forcebly constrayned,
> At Iuuynals request,
> To wryght of this glorious gest,
> Of this vayne gloryous best,
>
> . . . .
> *Quia difficile est*
> *Satiram non scribere.*

It would certainly have been difficult for Skelton not to write invective against Lord Thomas in the autumn of 1522 and into

the spring of 1523; and, in spite of his disclaimer, he may have
been spurred on also by his patrons to do so. *Why Come Ye?* was
written, for the most part, during this time—when England was
at war with France and under distressingly heavy taxation and
when popular feeling against Wolsey was at its peak.[124] This
situation is reflected with great clarity, as the poet—in his role
of *vates*, prophet, seer—rages at the absolute ruler:

> For wyll dothe rule all thynge,
> Wyll, wyll, wyll, wyll, wyll,
> He ruleth alway styll.
>
> . . . .
>
> There is no man but one
> That hathe the strokes alone;
> Be it blacke or whight,
> All that he dothe is ryght.

Wolsey is attacked for political wrongs and personal offenses, for
his ignorance (perhaps Skelton is not being quite fair here to
Oxford's famous "boy bachelor"), for the seven deadly and other
miscellaneous sins, for his exercise of witchcraft over the King,
for treachery, bribery, interference with judges, lawmakers,
churchmen. At the end, the poet pictures the Cardinal as a leper,
a victim of the pox, a Polyphemus with a diseased eye. And the
Latin summary following the English compilation again casti-
gates him as Namaan the leper.

Except that it is all aimed at Wolsey, the poem is not really
unified. Its seams are quite visible. The first passages are clearly
separated one from another by repeated refrains from old songs:
"In faythe, dycken, thou krew" (mentioned also in the *Bouge of
Court* and the *Devout Trental*) or "Mocke hath lost her sho." At
the end of another section, the poet concludes definitely, "But
now vpon this story / I wyll no further ryme / Tyll another
tyme, / Tyll another tyme." But the latter and longest part of
the "lytell boke" takes the form of a dialogue. A question is
asked: "What newes, what newes?"—and the journalist answers
in ballad-fashion, often at great length.

About midway through the poem, the key question occurs:
"Ones yet agayne / Of you I wolde frayne, / Why come ye nat
to court?" The poet counters: "To whyche court? / To the kynges

court, / Or to Hampton Court?" "Nay, to the kynges court," repeats the one eager for news. The laureate resumes, "The kynges
courte / Shulde haue the excellence; / But Hampton Court /
Hath the preemynence"—and the rest of the diatribe is a *cri de
coeur* telling why one no longer takes his proper place in the
affairs of state by coming to court.

It is interesting to note that in 1524–25, "stung perhaps by
Skelton's gibe," Wolsey "gave up" his lease on Hampton Court
to Henry, although he continued to live there until impeached.[125]
And it is significant of the wide hearing Skelton's "bold barke"
received that as late as May, 1527, the Spanish ambassador said
of Archbishop Warham that he was Wolsey's rival, an opponent
of the war with Spain—but "he never comes to court." [126]

At the end of the poem there is the laureate's cryptic number
xxxiiii, which has caused his critics trouble in dating the compilation. Nelson and Edwards, we recall, have determined that
Skelton's private calendar began in the autumn of 1488, although
he is not heard of in his official capacity until the following
spring. The mark xxxiiii, then, would set a *terminus ad quem*
of 1522 for *Why Come Ye?* Actually, this Procrustean bed will
not do. The poem is full of topical allusions, many of which have
not been identified. Some of them obviously refer to events that
took place before war was declared with France in May, 1522.
For example, the "countryinge at Cales" during which there was
much "Treatinge of trewse restlesse, / Pratynge for peace peas-
lesse," probably refers to Wolsey's fruitless but expensive mission
to Calais the preceding year. And Wolsey's notorious Star Chamber activities, mentioned often in the poem, began much earlier.
His edicts against the illiteracy of the nobility—the basis for
Skelton's lines,

> For all their noble blode
> He pluckes them by the hode,
>
> . . . .
>
> Theyr wyttes, he saith, are dull;
> He sayth they haue no brayne
> Theyr astate to mayntayne—

date from 1517; and his interference with judges and the law-
courts, described by Skelton in lines beginning, "Juges of the

kynges lawes, / He countys them foles and dawes," dates from
1517–18.[127]

Skelton helps to date his poem by saying that it is "within this
xvi. yere" since Wolsey was a chaplain "with a poore knyght"—
Sir Richard Nanfan, Deputy of Calais, who died in January, 1507.
The laureate was apparently writing, then, early in 1523. Certainly most of the events signaled by Skelton in the poem took
place in the years 1522–23.[128] Among those that can be accurately
dated as occurring in 1522 are London's election of a goldsmith
for mayor, Surrey's expedition to France, Wolsey's becoming
Abbot of St. Albans; the death of M. Meautys, the King's French
secretary, took place in March, 1523. In addition, the truce with
Scotland, arranged by Lord Dacre, was in effect during 1522–23;
and when Skelton laments

> Our royals that shone,
> Our nobles are gone
> Among the Burgonyons,
> And Spanyardes onyons,
> And the Flanderkyns.
>
> . . . .
> But Englande may well say,
>
> . . . .
> Now nothynge but pay, pay,
> With, laughe and lay downe,
> Borowgh, cyte, and towne,

he is referring to the fact that English money paid for war waged
by Charles V in the Lowlands—again, during 1522 and the following years.[129]

In April, 1523, Parliament was convened for the first time in
years in order to subsidize the war with France. But the session
was stormy, and Wolsey met great opposition to his plans for
taxation, especially when he himself invaded the House of Com-
mons to try to influence the members there.[130] A Tax Act was
eventually worked out, however, and it was during the following
months that resistance to the new taxes and tax collectors so
enraged the people that uprisings became imminent. Any number
of passages in *Why Come Ye?* could refer to these events—as

> He bereth the kyng on hand,
> That he must pyll his lande,

> To make his cofers ryche;
> But he laythe all in the dyche,
> And vseth suche abusyoun,
> That in the conclusyoun
> All commeth to confusyon.

And some of Skelton's invective seems to have been inspired by events that happened even later than 1523. One passage is especially revealing:

> In the regestry
> Of my Lorde of Cantorbury,
> To whom he was professed
>
> . . . .
>
> To be vnder his subiectyon:
> But now he maketh obiectyon,
>
> . . . .
>
> He makith so proude pretens,
> That in his equipolens
> He iugyth him equiualent
> With God omnipotent.

This reference is to Archbishop Warham, whose precincts Wolsey invaded (believing that as legate *a latere* he was a sort of resident pope in England with power to perform whatever functions he liked belonging to his subordinates or—as Professor Pollard puts it—his insubordinates) and who protested in 1519 and again in 1525.[131] And "Good Sprynge of Lanam" (Lavenham) is the subject of these lines referring to the Cardinal's tax laws: "My lordis grace wyll brynge / Downe this hye sprynge, / And brynge it so lowe, / It shall nat euer flowe." The wealthy wool merchant was the mediator between the tax commissioners and the insurgent people in 1525, when Lavenham was a center of disturbance.[132]

The composition of *Why Come Ye?* then, extended well into 1523, and parts of the poem may have been written even later.[133] The poem is not mentioned in the *Garland of Laurel* (to the great puzzlement of some of Skelton's interpreters) for the simple reason that it was not complete when the *Garland* (published October, 1523) was prepared for the press. And those who find it difficult to reconcile the laureate's seemingly mild attitude in the *Garland of Laurel* with his continuing invective against the Cardinal must have forgotten his witty *mot* of 1523 that echoed

throughout the land: "Gentle Paule laie doune thy swearde: / For
Peter of Westminster hath shauen thy beard."

This couplet was composed, we recall, when Wolsey recon-
vened the Archbishop's convocation (called simultaneously with
Parliament) from St. Paul's to Westminster in May, 1523; and it
was published by Hall in his account of the period. Skelton—
who could cast his wife out of his door at the Bishop's order and
take her back in through the window[134]—was expert in not letting
his left hand know what his right hand was doing. As for the
numeral xxxiiii following *Why Come Ye Not to Court?*, there are
several possible explanations. The number might apply to an
early part of the compilation. Or it might mean that Skelton's
appointment to the court of Henry VII did not actually take place
until the spring of 1489, rather than in the autumn of 1488.

The more one studies the Articles of Impeachment brought
against Wolsey a few months after Skelton's death, the closer
similarities one notices between this document and *Why Come
Ye Not to Court?* These forty-four articles finally presented to
the King by Sir Thomas More (the Lord Chancellor) and the
leading peers of the realm were drawn up from earlier lists of
charges kept by some of the petitioners.[135] In the light of these
striking similarities, it seems to me very likely that the old laureate's pointed invective was highly influential in bringing about
this final culmination of his arch-foe's fortunes in November,
1529, a few months after his own death. Thus Skelton not only
predicted Wolsey's fall: he apparently helped to bring it about.

i THE GARLAND OF LAUREL

Meantime, visiting in Yorkshire, Skelton had turned his hand
to another long poem, most of which harked back some decades
to the type of court poetry he had written as a young man. In
stately rhyme royal, set in the dream framework and replete with
all the trappings of allegory, this "Ryght Delectable Tratyse vpon
a Goodly Garlande or Chapelet of Laurell" [136] is polished verse,
very proper for a laureate. Significantly enough, the title of *orator
regius* is not mentioned in the superscription, which tells where
the poem was written (far indeed from court!) and emphasizes
the pleasant and enjoyable: "By Mayster Skelton, poete Laureat,
studyously dyuysed at Sheryfhotton Castell, in the Foreste of
Galtres, wherein ar comprysyde many and dyuers solacyous and

ryght pregnant allectyues of syngular pleasure, as more at large it doth apere in the proces folowynge."

Sometime toward the close of 1522, then, the poet was at Sheriff-Hutton Castle near York, having traveled north for the second time within the year or—as seems far more likely—having continued to stay at Sheriff-Hutton during 1521 (when he wrote *Speak, Parrot* while staying with the Howards) and for a year or two longer. Here, at any rate, he was the New Year's guest of the Countess of Surrey (whose husband, Thomas Howard, was away carrying on the King's war with France). Actually, it is tempting to speculate that Skelton is referred to as "her clerk" by the Countess because he was tutor to young Henry Howard (aged seven at the time the *Garland* was written), the future poet.[137] This would explain the poet's stay of several years in Yorkshire.

Hospitably entertained and made much over by the Countess and her ladies, the poet celebrates in his *Garland of Laurel* a very pretty and quite sincere gesture on the part of this feminine household. These ladies, the poet tells us, had embroidered a "cronell of lawrell with verduris light and darke," which the Countess had "deuysyd for Skelton, my clerke." The Countess continues, "For to his seruyce I haue suche regarde, / That of our bownte we wyll hym rewarde." The poet's description of these ladies "at their work" is a charming picture of the way gentlewomen spent their time during the winter in a cold, northern castle:

> Sume to enbrowder put them in prese,
>   Well gydyng ther glowtonn to kepe streit theyr sylk,
> Sum purlyng of goldde theyr worke to encrese
>   With fingers smale, and handis whyte as mylk;
>   With, Reche me that skane of tewly sylk;
> And, Wynde me that botowme of such an hew,
> Grene, rede, tawny, whyte, blak, purpill, and blew.

Occupation—who has presented Skelton to the Queen of Fame in the allegory—now suggests that the poet write a few lines to "theis ladys and gentylwomen all":

> In goodly wordes plesauntly comprysid,
> That for them some goodly conseyt be deuysid,

With proper captacyons of beneuolence,
  Ornatly pullysshid after your faculte,
. . . .
To iche of them rendryng thankis commendable,
With sentence fructuous and termes couenable.

And so the poet rewards the ladies, as they have rewarded
him; for about midway through the *Garland,* he pays tribute to
each of them in a series of poems. In rhyme royal he greets the
Countess—"So shall your name endure perpetually, / Whos pas-
syng bounte, and ryght noble astate, / Of honour and worship
it hath the formar date"—and three "ladies," members of the
Howard and Dacre families. These verses are filled with com-
parisons to famous ladies of former times.[138] But the laureate
abandons the rhyme-royal stanza for charming little lyrics in short
lines, sometimes ending with a refrain, when he honors the other
members of the household who were simple "mistresses." The
younger ladies are compared to flowers and birds, and each one
is thanked for her part in making the "chapelet."

Such is the actual occasion for the writing of the poem. But
this focal point is approached leisurely and conventionally, in
the best aureate style. There is an astrological beginning and a
dream in which the Queen of Fame reminds Dame Pallas "That
in my courte Skelton shulde haue a place, / Bycause that his
tyme he studyously hath spent / In your seruyce. . . ." As the
Queen of Fame continues, "But yet I beseche your grace that
good recorde / May be brought forth, suche as can be founde, /
With laureat tryumphe why Skelton sholde be crownde," the poet
is given an opportunity to prove his right to the laurel wreath.
There is a lengthy roll-call of poets laureate from "olde Quin-
tiliane"—here associated with Theocritus, Hesiod, and Homer—
up to such moderns as Gower, Chaucer, and Lydgate, who "wan-
tid [lacked] nothynge but the laurell" and who urge that Skelton
be employed in "our collage aboue the sterry sky." "Occupacyon,
Famys regestary," then leads the poet to the hall of the Countess
of Surrey, where dream and reality merge and where Skelton is
presented with his handsomely worked chaplet.

After Skelton's graceful verses to the ladies, his own bibliography appears in rhyme-royal stanzas, as *"Occupacyoun redith and
expoundyth sum parte of Skeltons bokes and baladis with ditis of*

plesure, *in as moche as it were to longe a proces to reherse all by name that he hath compylyd, &c."* Skelton's surviving works all have a place here, along with many that are not extant.[139] The allegory proper ends with a greeting to the New Year: "Good luk this new yere! the olde yere is past."

But the allegory has occasionally been interrupted—again, perhaps, in the style of the commonplace book—with Latin verse, a puzzle or two in Latin and English, Latin proverbs, short, non-rhyme-royal passages. And the list of Skelton's works is interrupted by the long apologia for *Philip Sparrow*, beginning, "For the gyse now adays / Of sum iangelyng iays / Is to discommende / That they can not amend." The poem concludes with Latin verses in praise of Skelton: *"Dicite, Skeltonis vester Adonis erat; / Dicite, Skeltonis vester Homerus erat."* There follows a graceful little envoy that supports Skelton's use of the English language:

> Go, litill quaire,
> Demene you faire;
> Take no dispare,
> Though I you wrate
> After this rate
> In Englysshe letter;
> So moche the better
> Welcome shall ye
> To sum men be. . . .

A second envoy, following a dedication to the King and to the Cardinal, reminds the legate *a latere* in Latin of the promise of a prebend and confesses in English, "Twene hope and drede / My lyfe I lede. . . ." These are the lines that have caused much bewilderment among Skelton's biographers and critics, who cannot reconcile this attitude with the anger and rage of the three long satires against Wolsey. Actually, neither the dedication nor the envoy appeared when the *Garland* was first published by Fawkes in 1523.[140] To this day, no one knows whether or not they were ever actually intended to follow the *Garland*, since they appeared for the first time in Marshe's edition of 1568. Surely the fact that Wolsey is conspicuously absent in the *Garland* need not mean that Skelton has suddenly, for some unaccountable reason, changed his mind about the Cardinal. Who would know

better than a poet laureate that in a poem aureate there is no
place for invective against Wolsey—in a poem written to justify
the poet to his good patroness, who has just presented "her clerk"
with a literal, richly devised symbol of his talents, service, and
accomplishments. Those who see in the *Garland* a supreme example of poetic egotism,[141] moreover, have certainly overlooked
both the purpose and the plan of the poem.

There is in the allegory, however, one section devoted to the
political scene, where "to this lady and souerayne of this palace /
Of purseuantis ther presid in with many a dyuerse tale; . . . /
With, How doth the north? what tydyngis in the sowth?" In the
midst of this lively scene Occupation gives a brief summary of
the poet's trials and labors, and promises him a peaceful old age:

> Of your aqueintaunce I was in tymes past,
>   Of studyous doctryne when at the port salu
> Ye fyrste aryuyd; whan broken was your mast
>   Of worldly trust, then did I you rescu;
>   Your storme dryuen shyppe I repared new,
> So well entakeled, what wynde that euer blowe,
> No stormy tempeste your barge shall ouerthrow.

Near the beginning of the *Garland,* Dame Pallas has already
commented on the difficulties of being an outspoken poet:

> For if he gloryously pullishe his matter,
> Then men wyll say how he doth but flatter;
>
> And if so hym fortune to wryte true and plaine,
>   As sumtyme he must vyces remorde,
> Then sum wyll say he hath but lyttill brayne,
>   And how his wordes with reason wyll not accorde. . . .

The laureate has "polished his matter" in many poems; he has
"written true and plain" in *Colin Clout;* he has found fault with
vices in all the great satires. In other words, he has been strenu-
ously occupied much of his life in behalf of the conservative party
of two reigns—and the protection and patronage of the Countess
are the rewards for "her clerk." We have seen evidence in *Speak,
Parrot* and elsewhere for the Countess' patronage. Actually, the
situation is quite similar in both poems—*Speak, Parrot* and the

Garland: in each one the laureate is the center of a feminine household, surrounded by the Countess and her ladies, who shower him with attentions. It is pleasant to think of the aging laureate in these peaceful surroundings during the last productive years of his life.

j THE DUKE OF ALBANY

No one knows how many poems Skelton composed in the years following the publication of the *Garland of Laurel* in 1523. Two occasional pieces, however, have come down to us: *The Douty Duke of Albany* and *A Replycacion agaynst Certayne Yong Scholers.* In these, Skelton leaves the lofty aureate style and returns to his own characteristic singing robes.

The first of these—"Howe the Douty Duke of Albany, Lyke a Cowarde Knyght, Ran Away Shamefully . . . Beside the Water of Twede, &c." [142]—is reminiscent of the earlier poems against the Scots, combining a news report with scurrilous invective. In short, clipped lines, the poet rails against Albany (who was regent of Scotland and led an unsuccessful border expedition against England in 1523), accusing him of treachery, cowardice, lying, deceit, stupidity, and ambitious desire to be King of Scotland, in rhymes that generate more rhymes:

> Yet ye dare do nothynge,
> But lepe away lyke frogges,
> And hyde you vnder logges,
> Lyke pygges and lyke hogges,
> And lyke maungy dogges.

At the same time, the poet glorifies England's defender (and Skelton's patron):

> Of chiualry the well,
> Of knighthode the floure
> In euery marciall shoure,
> The noble Erle of Surrey,
> That put thé in suche fray.

Having hammered away at the ignoble Duke—and, incidentally, having reported at great length on the campaign—the laureate now loyally turns to one who stands in great contrast to Albany, his own King, who is everything that a ruler should be: "Howe be it, loyally, / After myne allegyaunce, / My pen I will auaunce / To extoll his noble grace." This "royall regent," "pereless president," and "kyng most excellent" is compared to Hercules, Solomon, Absalom, Hector, Scipio, Ptolemy, and Joshua. His royal qualities are listed, one to a line in a magnificent catalogue; and the complete *rapport* between the monarch and his subjects is perhaps overstated:

> All his subiectes and he
> Moost louyngly agre
> With hole hart and true mynde,
> They fynde his grace so kynde;
> Wherwith he dothe them bynde
> At all houres to be redy
> With hym to lyue and dye.

At the end of the poem, the doughty Duke is threatened for his pride: "Auaunte, cowarde recrayed! / Thy pride shalbe alayd." And a brief envoy sums up the events described in the poem, beginning, "Go, lytell quayre, quickly; / Shew them that shall you rede, / How that ye are lykely / Ouer all the worlde to sprede."

k A REPLICATION

As the *orator regius* shows himself tremendously loyal to King and country in *The Douty Duke of Albany*, so his infinite loyalty to Mother Church informs the last poem from Skelton's pen, published in 1528, not long before his death: *A Replycacion Agaynst Certayne Yong Scolers Abiured of Late*.[143] Here the poet appears in his strongest persona: as a staunch supporter of the Church and as a violent opponent of anything faintly tinged with Lutheranism. The occasion for the poem was the public abjuration of heresy by two Cambridge lads who had been brought before the ecclesiastical court for their Protestant leanings. These scholars have been identified as Thomas Arthur and Thomas Bilney, who abjured their errors and, symbolically, carried faggots to Paul's Cross on December 8, 1527, to show publicly their renunciation of heresy. Arthur had quickly seen the error of his ways, and had abjured without hesitation; but Bilney was more difficult to deal with: he relapsed several years later and was burned in 1531.

What more suitable beginning, then, than a flowery Latin dedication to the legate *a latere,* the Pope's own representative in England? English prose mingles with Latin verse, as the laureate summarizes the heretical activities of the two scholars and commiserates with his own *alma universitas* in having produced two such sons. Skelton blames the encroachment of heresy on the laxness and shallowness of education, which allows young scholars to consider themselves clerks who have picked up only "A lytell ragge of rethorike, / A lesse lumpe of logyke, / A pece or a patche of philosophy."

In a long spasm of satirically bombastic prose (quite similar, actually, to the inflated, superficial, pseudo-learned language spoken by the university student whom Pantagruel meets in Rabelais' great novel—*Gargantua and Pantagruel* [Book II, Chapter VI]), Skelton explains the sins of the two scholars: ". . . that popholy and peuysshe presumpcion prouoked them to publysshe and to preche to people imprudent perilously, howe it was idolatry to offre to ymages of our blessed lady, or to pray and go on pylgrimages, or to make oblacions to any ymages of sayntes in churches or els where." Following this statement, the replication proper begins: "To the honour of our blessed lady, / And her most blessed baby, / I purpose for to reply / Agaynst this horryble heresy." The scholars are berated over and over in furious Skeltonics for their heretical leanings; and at the end they are advised "to forsake / Of heresy the deuyllysshe scoles, / And crye Godmercy, lyke frantyke foles."

The poem falls into three parts, of which the second is Skelton's answer to his own critics that poets are not suited to refuting heresy. His response is to call forth David, "that royall kyng," who combined poetry, prophesying, and governing so successfully, according to Saint Jerome:

> For Dauid, our poete, harped so meloudiously
> Of our Sauyour Christ in his decacorde psautry,
> That at his resurrection he harped out of hell
> Olde patriarkes and prophetes in heuen with him to dwell.

In a sincere little *apologia* for poetry and poets, Skelton proceeds
to reconcile the poet and the priest. Attributing to God the
"heuenly inspyracion" in "laureate creacyon," he explains that
"God maketh his habytacion / In poetes whiche excelles, / And
soiourns with them and dwelles." And he asks his readers for
understanding:

> Therfore no greuance,
> I pray you, for to take
> In this that I do make
> Agaynst these frenetykes,
> Agaynst these lunatykes,
> Agaynst these sysmatykes,
> Agaynst these heretykes,
> Nowe of late abiured.

The third and last part of the *Replication* is a set of Latin verses
on the scarcity of good poets ("rare and few are poets") compared to other learned types. An envoy addressed to the Cardinal
reminding him of the promise of "an ammas gray"—a church
office of some sort—seems to follow the poem.[144]

It has been pointed out that Skelton's *Replication* has many
parallels with Thomas More's prose *Dialogues Concerning Heresies,* written, like Skelton's poem, at the request of a prelate—
this time, Cuthbert Tunstall, Bishop of London.[145] Both works
probably represent, then, an official attempt to stamp out heresy
through all possible means—including rhetoric, eloquence. Skelton's vigorous response to this challenge was in no way a personal
capitulation to the Cardinal. It was simply his characteristic way
of putting first things first—of placing first the things of God and
of letting others follow.

CHAPTER 3

Essence

Innumeri sunt philosophi, sunt theologique,
Sunt infiniti doctores, suntque magistri
Innumeri, sed sunt pauci rarique poetae.

I *The Man*

a HUMANIST AND POET

THE late Professor Lewis has rightly observed of Skelton: "He
has no real predecessors and no important disciples; he stands
out of the streamy historical process, an unmistakable individual." [1] This individuality surely lies in the poet's position in time
and history—in the peculiar meeting of medieval and modern in
his training, background, thought, and character. Philip Henderson is clearly on the right track when he sees in Skelton's poetry
"the actual break-up of the Middle Ages" and when he views the
poet himself as "the last and peculiarly brilliant representative
of a great tradition, a man standing at a decisive turning point
of English culture and English history before the advent of
Humanism brought with it the flood of foreign and 'classical'
influences that has resulted in the neglect of our earlier poets
and the underestimation of our great medieval culture." [2]

A product of the encyclopedic university curriculum, based
largely upon the seven liberal arts and Aristotelian philosophy,
Skelton enjoyed an apparently brilliant academic career when an
occasional lecture in Greek might have been given at Oxford but
before the actual introduction of Greek into the Oxford curriculum. He became, then, a member of the first circle of English
humanists—the three or four at the court of Henry VII—although
his knowledge of Greek was slight, and was limited in his works
to an occasional word or phrase (especially in *Speak, Parrot,*
where it adds to the enigmatic character of the poem). But his
laureation or degree in rhetoric, an honor awarded only thrice in

Oxford's history,[3] was a distinction that Skelton cherished all his life and referred to more than once when his qualifications as a versifier were criticized—as in his flyting pieces with Garnesche. His knowledge of Latin literature, also everywhere apparent, is equaled only by his love of it. His own Latin poems, moreover, form a substantial part of the Skelton canon.

In the light of these interests and abilities it is not surprising that he began his public literary career as a translator, one worthy of Caxton's high standards and enthusiastic praise, and that he proceeded to indite verse in the formal aureate style, long conventional with such poets as Gower and Lydgate, Hawes and Barclay. Here, the aim was expansion in the most elegant verse, often in the rhyme-royal stanza. The Skelton read today, of course, is not the poet of the aureate tradition, the rhetorician skilled in polished versification.

But even in his early works, as we have seen, Skelton began to leave his individual mark upon English letters. And his translation of *Diodorus Siculus* introduced several hundred new words into the language of the day.[4] For like the Renaissance writers who followed him, Skelton had a tremendous interest in words, and could never get enough of their infinite variety. Unlike the typical English humanist, however, Skelton was first and last a poet, not a scholar; he was certainly not interested in textual criticism.[5] In fact, our laureate was the first English humanist to devote himself primarily to the writing of English verse, continually enriching his native tongue.

Skelton's humanism, then, was of a particular kind—one we might almost call old-fashioned. On the one hand, the poet was steeped in medieval scholasticism and to the end of his life thoroughly approved of dialectics. Much of his anger against the two Cambridge heretics (*A Replication*) and the irresponsible clergy (*Colin Clout*) springs from what he considered their ignorance of the terms and procedures of scholastic logic—enough to damn them forever in the old priest's eyes. Of "Doctour Daupatus" in *Colin Clout,* for instance, he says, "He can nothyng smatter / Of logyke nor scole matter, / Neyther *syllogisare,* / Nor *enthymemare. . . .*" Many passages, moreover, in *Speak, Parrot* decry the passing of the old learning ("Tryuyals and quatryuyals so sore now they appayre . . .").

Skelton's works might be called equally conservative in subject-matter: there is no reference whatever to new geographical or scientific discoveries, none of the secular Renaissance enthusiasms, no glimmer of understanding of Protestant views, no sign of the neo-Platonism that infuses, for example, Spenser's *Four Hymns* a half-century later. And, finally, Skelton's lack of enthusiasm for the study of Greek[6]—the language *par excellence* of Renaissance humanists—marks him as a conservative. Not that he objects to the study of Greek—"Yf it were cond perfytely, and after the rate, / As *lingua Latina*," he observes in *Speak, Parrot*. But in the same poem he complains that few scholars know enough Greek to be able to use it practically—that "they cannot say in Greeke, rydynge by the way, / How, hosteler, fetche my hors a botell of hay!"

In many ways, however, Skelton is a man of the Renaissance. The great strength and vigor of his works are Renaissance qualities, as are the complete self-confidence in his poetic abilities, pride in his official titles, and enjoyment of his fame—which, as he kept reminding his readers, was to be immortal. The Latin epigram preceding the *Garland of Laurel*, for example, shows the laureate far removed from medieval conventions, whereby a poet humbly and modestly apologized for his lack of skill; and later in the same poem he proudly directs his songs to celebrate him as Britain's Adonis, as England's Homer: "*Dicite, Skeltonis vester Adonis erat; / Dicite, Skeltonis vester Homerus erat. . . .*" Here is true Renaissance ebullience—the same quality that informs much of what Skelton wrote and that constantly shows itself in his great love for his native language, his utter intolerance of hypocrisy, his independence in life as well as writings, his glorying in the robust and the vulgar, his strong sense of the comic, his penetrating wit, and—except when lambasting the Cardinal —his good humor. In all these qualities, indeed, Skelton aligns himself unmistakably with his great counterparts a generation later on the Continent who also gloried in the vernacular and held that laughter is proper for mankind—François Rabelais and the Italian Folengo.

The old laureate's opinion of himself has been at least somewhat justified through the years and has been richly repaid in modern times. And it is not by accident that his fame rests, not on his serious works written in rhyme royal, but on the lighter verse-form named for him. Just what is "Skeltonic verse"? Much

has been written on this subject and various theories have been
put forth as to how it originated—whether from the medieval
tradition of rhymed Latin prose (*Reimprosa*), which Skelton's
own *Speculum principis* follows in part, from medieval hymn
forms, or from some other source.[7]

In certain respects, one might almost call the Skeltonic form-
less; and yet its chief characteristics are so plainly marked that
even those who cannot write "poetry" can get off a burst of
Skeltonics on occasion. There are short lines—lines containing
two, three, or four beats. And there is unending rhyme—but
never cross-rhyme—in lines that often seem to be self-perpetuat-
ing. There are alliteration and repetition and parallelism; there
are punning and witticism and much sprinkling of Latin. More
subtly and very musically, there is the mingling of accent and
quantity, as long beats are accented and short ones are adjusted
between the stresses. The opening spondees of *Philip Sparrow*
show this adjustment put to most effective use: *"Pla-ce-bo / Who
is there who?"* But whatever its origin and whatever its Con-
tinental analogues (the *fratrasie* in France, the *frottola* in Italy),
Skeltonic verse in the last analysis is based ineluctably upon the
natural rhythms of English speech.[8]

Interestingly enough, in originating and developing this form,
Skelton singled out the strongest characteristic of medieval poetry
—amplification, expansion, the art of saying the same thing in
many different ways—and put it to new and unorthodox use. If
to the old principle of expansion be added Skelton's personal
genius for inventiveness—that division of rhetoric concerned with
the amplification of themes—combined with his deeply satirical
wit, amazing facility with words, and keen ear for musical
rhythms, the Skeltonic becomes inevitable. The Skeltonic, then,
is the peculiar result of an old medieval principle put to a new
and highly personal use by an unorthodox, forward-looking poet.

b MUSICIAN

It is everywhere obvious in his poetry that Skelton thinks in
musical rhythms. Even in his rhyme-royal poetry, as already
noted, his lines often sing themselves musically in a basic four-
beat meter, rather than in the conventional pentameter of that
verse form. Two examples from his works will make this musical
quality abundantly clear. Of many possible choices, let us com-

pare two stiff, dignified pentameter lines from an early lyric—
"Knolege, aquayntance, resort, fauour with grace; / Delyte, de-
syre, respyte with lyberte"—with these sparkling lines about the
"comely coistrown," where the five feet are adjusted to a basic
four-beat meter (sometimes with upbeat), exactly as though one
were setting the words to music in quarter notes and eighth notes:
(2/4) "*Comely* he *clap*pyth a *payre* of clauy*cordys;* / He *whyste*-
lyth so *swetely* he *makyth* me to *swete.*" The English predilection
for regular or "square" melodies has long been known—melodies
made up of strains of four plus four measures. Much of Skelton's
verse bears out this trend.

But Skelton's use of music is by no means limited to rhythmic
subtleties: his works are filled with musical references of many
different kinds. Some of these are allusions to sacred music, and
most of them are found in *Philip Sparrow* and in the two long
satires on ecclesiastical evils (*Colin Clout* and *Why Come Ye
Not to Court?*). *Philip Sparrow,* as already noted, is set in the
frame of the Requiem Mass and Office; and Skelton not only
quotes from this liturgy freely (separating the syllables) but
even writes out the musical syllables ("*fa, re, mi, mi*") to heighten
the effect of thinking aloud, of humming bits of song. Quotations
from the Gregorian chant are marvelously apt—as "*De pro fun
dis cla ma vi,* / Whan I sawe my sparowe dye!*" What better way
to make poignant the reaction of a little girl than to relate the
words of the Penitential Psalm, "Out of the depths have I cried
unto Thee" (a part of the Burial Service), to the death of a
sparrow!

In *Colin Clout,* snatches from the Gregorian chant are effectively inserted to point up discrepancies between the clergy as
they are and as they should be. The word *Sitientes* ("thirsty
ones"), the first word of the Introit of the Mass for Passion Sunday ("Sitientes, venite ad aquas, dicit Dominus"), for example,
brings powerful overtones, as Skelton piles up Latin rhymes and
berates ignorant, neglectful priests, thirsty for anything but the
living waters:

> As at *Sitientes,*
> Some are *insufficientes,*
> Some *parum sapientes,*
> Some *nihil intelligentes,*

Some *valde negligentes,*
Some *nullum sensum habentes.* . . .

In the same poem, the satire is greatly strengthened by mention of a popular sequence sung at Lady-Mass, as the poet complains "Howe some synge *Lætabundus:*[9] / At euery ale stake," and proceeds to blast away at priests who keep women. Similarly, in *Why Come Ye?* he ends a section on the Cardinal's "willful blindness"—both spiritual and physical—with an allusion to chanting "from blindness of heart, deliver us, O Lord": "*A cæcitate cordis,* / In the Latyne synge we, / *Libera nos, Domine!*" And how more effectively could he underline the Cardinal's pomposity and self-importance than by quoting the beginning of an antiphon ("Lo, the great priest") sung at Mass and other services of a Confessor Bishop: "*Ecce, sacerdos magnus,* / That wyll hed vs and hange vs, / And streitly strangle vs. . . ."

Equally effective for characterization and even more numerous than phrases from the ecclesiastical chant are short quotations from popular songs that appear in many of the poems. Unlike the sacred chants, however, parts of popular songs are found for the most part in the lighter poems; and they may be anything from a few nonsense words—like "Hey trolly lolly!"[10]—to entire refrains. It is possible to find at least twenty of these, some of them used twice, some three times in the poems. We have already noted the introduction of the Flemish dance-tune *Roti boulli joyeulx* in the poem *Against a Comely Coistrown.* In the *Bouge of Court,* Harvy Hafter names a popular song he would like to be able to sing, although he cannot read music ("sing on the book"): "Prynces of yougthe can ye synge by rote? . . . / For on the booke I can not synge a note." The opening line of this chanson begins the refrain in the lyric to the Lady Anne Dacre in the *Garland of Laurel:* both stanzas of this little poem end with the lines, "Princes of youth, and flowre of goodly porte, / Vertu, conyng, solace, pleasure, comforte." And the second phrase of the chanson ("flowre of godlihede") forms part of the refrain to the little lyric addressed "*To mastres Margery Wentworthe,*" beginning, "With margerain ientyll, / The flowre of goodlyhede." *Princess of youth,* which survives in a three-part anonymous setting in an Escorial manuscript, was one of the earliest English songs to become popular on the Continent.[11] This popularity is attested to by Skelton's use of it: first, as a fashionable piece of music to be associated with Harvy Hafter; and also for its lovely words, suitable for application to a charming young lady.

To choose only one other example, we may note the scene in *Magnificence* following the stage direction that brings in Courtly Abusion singing: "*Hic ingrediatur* Courtly Abusyon *cantando.*" [12] After he sings a bit of the Flemish melody, "Rutty bully, ioly rutterkyn, heyda!," Courtly Abusion is asked by Cloaked Collusion, "*De que pays este vous?* . . . / Say [savey] *vous chaunter Venter tre dawce?*" To this question Abusion replies in French, "*Wyda, wyda* [oui-da]." Just as *Roti bouilli* brings overtones of the fashionable "rutterkin," so mention of *Votre très douce*—a chanson by Gilles Binchois (d. 1460)—calls up French associations. Both songs, in other words, heighten in this scene the air of dandyism, of newfangled fashions, of the upstart courtier with his affected, foreign airs.

Skelton refers to above a dozen musical instruments, some of them a number of times; and he invariably shows a genuine technical acquaintance with them. Each time the choice is obviously a deliberate one—for some special effect or special characterization. Sometimes alliteration sets the pattern, as "Comely he clappyth a payre of clauycordys" or "He lumbryth on a lewde lewte" (*Against a Comely Coistrown*). But the most interesting fact that emerges from a study of Skelton's musical images is the consistency with which he finds the same instrument apt for certain effects —sometimes good, sometimes bad. Trumpets sound often and triumphantly throughout the *Garland of Laurel*, for instance, as the poet noisily calls attention to his own accomplishments. There is onomatopeia ("bararag") when Dame Pallas directs the Queen of Fame to see that Skelton laureate is properly announced:

> Call forthe, let se where is your clarionar,
> To blowe a blaste with his long breth extendid;
> Eolus, your trumpet, that knowne is so farre,
> That bararag blowyth in euery mercyall warre,
> Let hym blowe now. . . .

The harp represents for Skelton the poetic gift ("My penne nowe wyll I sharpe," he says in *Colin Clout*, "And wrest vp my harpe / With sharpe twynkyng trebelles"); and it is consistently associated with Apollo, Orpheus, and other musicians from antiquity, with King David, and with heavenly harmony.[13]

The fiddle, however, has quite different associations, which, heightened by alliteration, Skelton turns to his own characteristic usage in a bit of satire against an adversary (*Garland of Laurel*): "And what blunderar is yonder that playth didil diddil? / He fyndith fals mesuris out of his fonde fiddill." Similarly, he characterizes the Comely Coistrown—"A master, a mynstrell, a fydler, a farte." Even sharper is his likening of an old woman to a *rebibe* or rebec (a small, high-pitched ancestor of the violin) in *Elinor Rumming:* "There came an old rybybe / She halted of a kybe."

One of the instruments that appears in the poem *Against a Comely Coistrown* is the monochord: "But ask wher he fyndyth among hys monacordys / An holy water clarke a ruler of lordys." This one-string instrument was used, not for performance, but for teaching purposes in choir schools—for demonstration of string divisions and laws of musical acoustics; and Skelton himself must have been thoroughly familiar with it. He reveals a remarkable knowledge of the technical side of music throughout this same poem, for the upstart musician is ridiculed in technical musical terms with puns so obvious—and so popular with later Renaissance writers—that they need no glossing nowadays. Skelton, in fact, runs the whole gamut here of musical terminology, with *rest, rule, space, solfa, treble, base* (*bass*), *measure, counter, descant, mean, discord, wrest, proportion, pricksong, plainsong, large, long, feign.*

Musical syllables used in sight-singing (*ut, re, mi, fa, sol, la*) appear many times in Skelton's poems, not only to indicate melodies from the Gregorian chant (as throughout *Philip Sparrow*) but also for humorous purposes of characterization. In the *Bouge of Court*, Harvy Hafter, who would like to sing because singing is fashionable, inadvertently refers to the sometimes harsh habits of singing teachers, we recall, when, after confessing that he cannot sing a note "on the book," he asks that someone "lerne me to synge . . . / And, whan I fayle, bobbe me on the noll." The medieval hexachord system[14] lies behind Skelton's facetious characterization in terms of the musical syllables. Unless one knows, for example, that e-*la* was the highest note in this scale, one misses the significance of Skelton's lines about the ambitious but untalented ostrich in the catalogue of birds in *Philip Sparrow* where the birds are described in human—and generally clerical —terms. Of the ostrich we read,

> He can not well fly
> Nor synge tunably
> Yet at a brayde
> He hath well assayde
> To solfe aboue ela. . . .

Similarly, the reference to a-*la-mi-re* in *Colin Clout* signifies a very high note in the gamut (and, of course, gives Skelton another rhyme). Here Colin remarks of bishops,

> They make but lytell sure,
> And meddels [sic] very lyght
> In the Churches ryght;
> But *ire* and *venire*,
> And solfa so alamyre,
> That the premenyre [praemunire]
> Is lyke to be set a fyre. . . .

Skelton's line marks the earliest known use of a-*la-mi-re* in literature; and this fact is also true of several other technical musical terms: *gamut, harp* (as a verb), *part* in a musical sense (see *Magnificence* [l. 1481]: "I synge of two partys without a mene"), *harmony* (meaning a pleasing combination of sounds), *quibible* (quinible, a fifth voice above the tenor), and still others in *Diodorus Siculus*.[15]

From the realm of musical ideas, finally, Skelton draws upon the age-old story of Orpheus and the power of music to move men, beasts, trees, and rocks. This well-known story is part of the dream sequence in the *Garland of Laurel;* but Skelton gives it a unique and humorous twist by having the very tree-stump against which he leaned respond to the music. In his dream, Skelton heard a "murmur of mynstrels," among whom

> Orpheus, the Thraciane, herped meledyously [sic]
> Weth Amphion, and other Musis of Archady;
> . . . .
> The huge myghty okes them selfe dyd auaunce,
> And lepe frome the hylles to lerne for to daunce:

> In so moche the stumpe, whereto I me lente,
> Sterte all at ones an hundrethe fote backe. . . .

From the world of sacred literature Skelton has drawn another
example of the power of music to sway men's souls. The last part
of *A Replication* becomes, we recall, a defense of the poet as
judge of theological matters—obviously in response to some criticism of Skelton's stand against the heretical students. In true
scholastic fashion, Skelton cites as authority for his qualifications
the statement of St. Jerome about David's powers as poet and
musician and then he pays tribute to David's miraculous music.[16]

Skelton's verse, then, is permeated with musical statement and
metaphor drawn from various divisions of music known to the
medieval scholar: musical theory and practice, sacred and secular
music, and musical ideas. In finding musical imagery especially
apt for characterization, punning, and witticism of many kinds,
Skelton is remarkably like Rabelais a generation later; indeed,
some of their allusions are practically identical.[17] Far more than
Rabelais, however, Skelton shows himself everywhere in touch
with practical musical matters—with musical services in the
church and the chanting of the liturgy for various occasions, with
the training for that type of service, and with secular musical
practices both instrumental and poetic. There is little evidence
that Skelton ever "read music" in depth at any university; and
there is no evidence at all that he knew the *Musica* of Boethius,
the standard text in music in university lecture halls for centuries.[18] But his practical knowledge of music is everywhere paramount.

It seems more than reasonable to conclude, then, that Skelton
received his secondary education as a scholar in a choir school
somewhere in England.[19] And as a student in the university, he
would have studied music as well as the other disciplines of the
quadrivium (arithmetic, astronomy, and geometry) before proceeding bachelor of arts. Later, as tutor to the future King,
Skelton may have had an important part in shaping the musical
studies of this young boy destined to become famous for his
musical abilities and compositions.[20] It is not unlikely, moreover,
that the laureate himself was a lutenist. At any rate, Erasmus
addressed to him a laudatory poem couched in musical metaphor,

which, if meant to be taken literally as well as figuratively, praised Skelton's skill on the lute.[21]

At court, Skelton was intimately associated with at least two distinguished musicians. One of these, William Cornish[22]—successively Master of the Singing-Boys of Westminster Abbey, Gentleman of the Chapel Royal, and Master of the Children of the Chapel Royal—was in charge of music for plays and pageants at court. It was he who took the Chapel Royal (the King's private choir) to France with Henry VIII, winning great favor by its performance at Thérouenne, Lille, and Tournai. Robert Pen, Gentleman of the Chapel and another of Skelton's musical friends —the *Diodorus Siculus* is addressed to him—also accompanied Henry in 1520 to the Field of the Cloth of Gold. Skelton's *Chorus de Dis* against the French and against the Scots, performed during this campaign, would have been under Cornish's direction. And Skelton's association with the composer paid off handsomely, as we have seen, when Cornish set several of the laureate's secular, robust lyrics for the Gentlemen of the Chapel to sing.

In 1504, Cornish was in Fleet Prison—because of a satirical poem on Sir William Empson, according to Stow's *Annals*. While languishing in jail, Cornish wrote a poem in musical terms called "A Treatise between Truth and Information," which is printed in Marshe's edition of Skelton's *Pithy, Pleasant and profitable works,* 1568 (and also in Davis' 1736 reprint of this edition).[23] "A. B. of E. how C. for T. was P. in P.," Cornish heads his poem (A Book of [?] how Cornish for Truth was Put in Prison?). Close reading of these stanzas reveals an extremely uneven style. The better parts, however, show remarkable similarities to Skelton's techniques. The laureate may well have lent his talents to helping a friend in jail state his case in verse and in musical metaphor in order to get the King's ear—which seems to have been the purpose of the poem.

In our own day, Skelton's great musical interests have been spendidly repaid by the late Ralph Vaughan Williams, whose choral-orchestral suite called *Five Tudor Portraits, A Choral Suite founded on Poems by John Skelton (Laureate)*,[24] is a brilliant setting in five parts: Ballad, "The Tunning of Elinor Rumming"; Intermezzo, "My pretty Bess"; Burlesca, "Epitaph on John Jaybeard of Diss"; Romanza, "Jane Scroop (her lament for Philip

Sparrow)"; and Scherzo, "Jolly Rutterkin." Vigorous and robust,
or pensive and lyrical, the music throughout reflects the tone of
the poetry. Especially interesting is the introduction of bits of
the sequence *Dies irae* (sung at the burial services) in the Romanza (*Philip Sparrow*). The musical notes to the second phrase
of the sequence ("*dies illa*") fit Skelton's quotation "*fa, re, mi,
mi*"—and Dr. Vaughan Williams has cleverly adjusted his setting
to correspond. The middle section of the Romanza is remarkable
for the variety of bird calls expressed in the music. Quotations
from the Requiem Mass and Office are sometimes set in the free
style of the Gregorian chant, as a sort of descant to the ordinary
four-part setting of the rest of the poem being sung at the same
time.

II *The Reputation and Influence*

Vaughan Williams' magnificent tribute to the laureate is a
significant indication of Skelton's position nowadays. For the
poet's reputation is higher today than at any time, except, perhaps, during his own lifetime and in the years immediately following. But Skelton's reputation has undergone many changes
since his death four and a half centuries ago. In his own day, he
was highly regarded as a rhetorician. Caxton, we recall, praised
him as a translator (1490), as one who wrote "in polysshed and
ornate termes craftely." About the same time, Erasmus praised
him in a lengthy eulogy and referred to him in a dedication to
Prince Henry as "that incomparable light and ornament of British letters." Robert Whittington, himself an Oxford laureate,
addressed a long ode to his fellow poet in 1519, praising Skelton
as the glory of English poets.[25]

There were some exceptions, however, among Skelton's admir-
ing contemporaries. One was Alexander Barclay, who in his *Ship
of Fools* (1509) had spoken derogatorily of *Philip Sparrow*, as
being light and frivolous and unworthy of a serious poet (and
Skelton had got his own back at such "jangling jays" in his
Garland of Laurel). Barclay's *Fourth Eclogue*, a paraphrase of
Mantuan's fifth eclogue "treating of the behauour of Riche men
agaynst Poetes," contains a blast against "rascalle poets" that has
generally been considered a diatribe against Skelton in particular,
beginning, "Then is he decked as Poet laureate, / When stinking
Thais made him her graduate." [26] According to Bale, Barclay

wrote a whole work of some sort *Contra Skeltonum.*[27] If he did
so, the book has long since disappeared. The distinguished schoolmaster and grammarian, William Lyly, who also regarded Skelton
with great disfavor, left a witty epigram to show it (1520)—apparently a reply to a similar poem by Skelton against Lyly. In
the words of Thomas Fuller,

> *William Lilly* was the School-master, whom he fell foul with, though
> gaining nothing thereby, as may appear by his return. And this I will
> do for *W. Lilly,* (though often beaten for his sake) endeavour to
> translate his answer:

> With face so bold, and teeth so sharp
> Of Vipers venome, why dost carp?
> Why are my verses by thee weigh'd
> In a false scale? may truth be laid?
> Whilst thou to get the more esteem
> A *learned Poet* fain wouldst seem;
> *Skelton* thou art, let all men know it,
> Neither learned, nor a Poet.[28]

Barclay apparently resented the morals of the Rector of Diss,
as well as his frivolity in verse-making. Ironically, however, "religious Barclay" and "inventive Skelton" share a tribute from Henry
Bradshaw ("sometyme monke in Chester," according to his prologue), whose *Saint Werburge* (published in 1521, though written earlier: Bradshaw died in 1513) concludes with some verses,
beginning, "Go forth litell boke / Jesu be thy spede":

> Fyrst to maister Chaucer / and Ludgate sentencious
> Also to preignaunt Barkley / nowe beyng religious
> To inuentive Skelton and poet laureate
> Praye them all of pardon both erly and late[29]

The same hagiologist in his *Life of Saint Radegund* (1521) speaks
in one breath of Chaucer and Skelton as "fathers of eloquens." [30]
Bradshaw, then, apparently had a high regard for the serious
poet. And a glance at the editions of Skelton's poetry published
in the period following his death show that from the mid-century
onward he enjoyed a wave of popularity that culminated in the
collected edition of his poems published by Thomas Marshe in

1568: *Pithy pleasaunt and profitable workes of maister Skelton, Poete Laureate.*[31] Prefixed to this edition were verses by Thomas Churchyard, summarizing briefly the history of poetry and giving a roll call of worthy poets: many highly laudatory lines are devoted to Skelton.[32] We recall, too, that Skelton's reputation as a "merry poet" was such that Edward Hall in his history of the Tudors (*The Union of the Two Noble and Illustre Famelies of Lancastre and York* [1548]) could quote a witty epigram made by the laureate against Wolsey's meddling with the clergy in 1523. Raphael Holinshed cited this verbatim—with a reference to Hall—in his *Chronicles of England, Scotlande, and Irelande,* published in 1587; and he also listed Skelton, "a pleasant poet," with other "lerned men" of the reign of Henry VIII.[33]

A diversity of opinion may be seen toward the end of the century when Skelton is noticed in surveys of English literature. William Webbe, in his *Discourse of English Poetrie* (1586), praises Chaucer and Lydgate, and then continues: "Since these I knowe none other tyll the time of *Skelton,* who writ in the time of kyng *Henry* the eyght, who as indeede he obtayned the Lawrell-Garland, so may I wyth good ryght yeelde him the title of a Poet: hee was doubtles a pleasant conceyted fellowe, and of a very sharpe wytte, exceeding bolde, and would nyppe to the very quicke where he once sette holde."[34]

George Puttenham, however, in his *Arte of English Poesie* (1589), expresses a very adverse opinion apparently based entirely on the poems written in Skeltonics, for he says nothing about the serious, aureate verse—very much out of fashion, of course, at the time Puttenham wrote. Puttenham's first notice of Skelton is derogatory, in his listing of English poets: ". . . then in king *Henry* th' eight times *Skelton,* (I wot not for what great worthines) surnamed the poet *Laureat.*"[35] Later, speaking of "Carols and rounds and such light or lasciuious Poemes, which are commonly more commodiously vttered by these buffons or vices in playes then by any other person," he is extremely harsh in his judgment: "Such were the rimes of *Skelton* (vsurping the name of a Poet Laureat) being in deede but a rude rayling rimer and all his doings ridiculous, he vsed both short distaunces and short measures pleasing onely the popular eare: in our courtly maker we banish them vtterly."[36]

Francis Meres, in his *Palladis Tamia* of 1598, echoes Puttenham in denigrating the old laureate: "*Skelton* (I know not for what great worthines, surnamed the Poet Laureat) applied his wit to scurrilities and ridiculous matters, such among the Greeks were called *Pantomini*, with us *Buffons*." [37] And Henry Peacham, in *The Compleat Gentleman* (1622), echoes these writers; but he does refer the curious to one of the laureate's serious works, probably because he had seen the original still hanging in West-minster's Lady Chapel. For in his account of English poets, Peacham mentions "Skelton, a poet laureate, for what desert I could never hear. If you desire to see his vein and learning, an epitaph upon King Henry the Seventh at Westminster will dis-cover it." [38]

What appeared to be buffoonery to the serious critic, however, seemed highly desirable to the writer of comedy; and so the laureate had many imitators throughout the century and beyond. The anonymous school play *Thersites* (c. 1537), written in short Skeltonic lines, so resembles in tone and style Skelton's lighter works that its author could only have been someone consciously imitating him. [39] Another anonymous Tudor play, the *Interlude of Youth* (c. 1560), echoes the *Bouge of Court* and also *Magnifi-cence*, when a character called Riot enters and speaks: "Huffa! huffa! who calleth after me? / I am Riot, full of jollity. / My heart is light as the wind, / And all on riot is my mind." [40]

Attention has already been called to the mention of Doctor Dawcocke (from *Ware the Hawk*) in Robert Greene's *Friar Bacon and Friar Bungay* (c. 1591). Actually, Skelton's shadow hovers over all the academic scenes in this play (especially II, iv, and III, ii), heightening the humor. For Greene very cleverly has Miles, "Friar Bacon's poor scholar," speak many lines in Skel-tonics—macaronic lines, at that, combining English and Latin, as befits a scholar. Ben Jonson, too, found the less serious side of Skelton worthy of imitation. In his masque, *The Fortunate Isles* (1626), Jonson has "skipping Skelton" appear and recite lines from *Elinor Rumming*. And Elinor herself dances in the anti-masque here, along with another famous hostess known to the laureate, Long Meg of Westminster. Earlier, one of Jonson's collaborators, Anthony Munday, had introduced Skelton in his play *The Downfall of Robert Earl of Huntington* (1601). And in Samuel Rowley's play *When You See Me, You Know Me* (1606), Skelton had been associated with Will Sommers. Near the beginning of the play, Dudley replies to King Henry's question as to the whereabouts of Will Sommers, his Fool: "He was met my liege they say at London / Earely this morning with Doctor Skelton"; and the King comments, "Hes never from him."

Imitation of Skelton, however, was not limited to drama. Soon after the defeat of the Armada, there was printed in London (for Toby Cooke, 1589) "A Skeltonical *Salutation*"—in Latin and English—beginning, "O King of Spaine / Is it not a paine . . . / To see thy traine / For to sustaine . . . / The worlds disdaine." Some years later, the poet Michael Drayton left among his odes (1627) an unfinished *Skeltoniad*. This brief poem about poems and poets, however, imitates the laureate very poorly and, except for the title, makes no mention of him.[41]

Perhaps Skelton's most enduring fame was as a polemicist. Ironically enough, as the Reformation became widespread, the bitter invective that the orthodox old priest had hurled against Cardinal Wolsey (especially in *Colin Clout*) was now imitated and used as a weapon by the Reformers. Even while Skelton was writing his last savage outburst against the Cambridge heretics, the renegade authors of the poem *Rede Me and Be Nott Wrothe* (1528) were echoing his charges against the Cardinal as proof that Wolsey himself was a heretic.[42] Later in the century, there were countless echoes of *Colin Clout* in the great body of poetry that resulted from religious controversy. Some of this verse imitated Skelton so closely that it was long attributed to him—for example, the lengthy *Image of Ipocrisy* and the *Vox Populi, Vox Dei*,[43] in which the common people address their grievances to the King.

But the name Colin Clout came to stand generally for the simple critic from among the lay people, whether interested in religious or other reforms. "Collyn clowte" is spokesman, for example, in a humorous controversy over the wearing of beards (1543); he upholds the affirmative side on the excellence of these excrescences, as against negative views set forth by the Rabelaisian medical doctor, Andrew Borde (*Borde on Berdes*, 1542).[44] Best known of all, however, is Spenser's immortalizing the name for his "simple shepherd boy," spokesman for the poet himself in the *Shepheardes Calender* (1579) and in *Colin Clouts Come Home Againe* (1595).[45]

By the end of the century, then, Skelton the polemicist had

been taken over by his arch-enemies, the Protestants. And his reputation was generally low as the Renaissance drew to a close, if we can believe Webbe and Peacham. Even so, *Elinor Rumming* continued to be popular enough to merit one printing in 1609, two in 1624. Shortly after the Restoration, the laureate found an honorable place among Fuller's *Worthies* (1662), in which the information is more biographical than literary. Fuller cites Erasmus' praise of Skelton (*"Britannicarum Literarum Lumen et Decus"*) and then says, "Yet was his Satyrical wit unhappy to light on *three Noli me tangere's*, viz. the *rod* of a *Schoolmaster*, the *Couls* of *Friars*, and the *Cap* of a *Cardinal*. The *first* gave him a *lash*, the *second* deprived him of his *livelyhood*, and the *third* almost outed him of his *life*." [46] Fuller then explains Skelton's falling out with Lyly, his running controversy with the friars, and his involvement with Wolsey; and he also recounts the legend of Skelton's keeping a concubine. [47] A couple of decades later, Anthony à Wood included Skelton in his *Athenae Oxonienses* (1691), drawing largely upon Bale and Fuller and concluding, ". . . yet the generality said, that his witty discourses were biting, his laughter opprobrious and scornful, and his jokes commonly sharp and reflecting." [48]

The eighteenth century saw the beginning of a rise in Skelton's reputation that has continued, for the most part, until the present. At the height of the Augustan period, oddly enough, a reprint of *Elynour Rummyng* appeared (1718), prefaced by an unusual defense of the poem. The editor states that "this Piece of Antiquity" has not been revived for those "whose chief Perfections is to discover the fine turn in a new Epilogue. . . ."

But Persons of an extensive Fancy and just Relish, who can discover Nature in the lowest Scene of life, and receive pleasure from the meanest Views; who prie into all the Variety of Places and Humours at present, and think nothing unworthy their Notice; . . . it is in Respect to them, and for a Moment's Amusement that this merry Old Tale is reviv'd. The Subject is low, it's true; and so is Chaucer's Old Widow; yet the Description of her Hovel pleases as much in it's Way, as a more lofty Theme. [49]

In 1736, the Marshe edition of Skelton's poems was reprinted for the first time since 1568. It was probably this collection that Pope had in mind when in his "Epistle to Augustus" he penned

his famous couplet seemingly excoriating Chaucer and Skelton—
but actually complimenting the laureate by emphasizing his perennial popularity with diners at high tables in college communi-
ties: "Chaucer's worst ribaldry is learned by rote, / And beastly
Skelton Heads of houses quote."

The *Bouge of Court*, not heard of for some time now, received
enthusiastic praise from Mrs. Elizabeth Cooper in *The Muses'
Library* (1741).[50] More important, the first comprehensive treatment of Skelton appeared in 1778 in Thomas Warton's volumi-
nous *History of English Poetry*.[51] Although Warton followed
Puttenham and Meres in regarding much of Skelton's verse as
low and vulgar ("It is in vain to apologize for the coarseness,
obscenity, and scurrility of Skelton, by saying that his poetry is
tinctured with the manners of his age. Skelton would have been
a writer without decorum at any period"), he carefully analyzes
the long poems and occasionally finds something to praise—for
instance, the "little sonnets" to the ladies in the *Garland of
Laurel*. Warton's final judgment is mixed ("No writer is more
uneven than Skelton"); he praises the laureate's Latin poems and
stresses (disapprovingly) one of the poet's strongest and today
most admired traits—his Goliardic propensities.

The early nineteenth century saw Skelton's works in *Chalmers'
English Poets* in 1810, the first American edition in 1819, and
favorable mention by Robert Southey in 1831 (*Select Works of
the British Poets*). Wordsworth, we recall, had echoed him in
a sonnet of 1806. Strongest praise of anyone up to this time, however, came from the unlikely pen of Elizabeth Barrett Browning
(1842), who with great insight singled out immediately Skelton's
strongest characteristic—his power and forcefulness—and saw
him as an "influence for good upon our language." [52] The year
1843 saw the publication of the splendid critical edition of Skelton's works by the Reverend Alexander Dyce, and the old laureate had an assured place in the world of letters.

Toward the end of the century, German philologists began to
study Skelton's poetry in depth. In New England, the Dyce edition was reprinted many times before 1900. Ramsay's critical
edition of *Magnificence* appeared in 1908, awakening interest in
the laureate as dramatist. During the 1920's, selected works began to appear in separate editions and in collections. The world
of academe was attracted to Skelton, universities took him up,

and articles about him found their way into the scholarly jour-
nals. The 1930's saw Philip Henderson's first edition of Skelton's
complete works in modern dress and the first of the biographies,
which continue to appear.

A good deal of the credit for contemporary appreciation of
Skelton is due to Robert Graves, who has done much to bring
him before the public. In *The Crowning Privilege* (1955), based
upon the Clark Lectures delivered at Cambridge in 1954, Graves
takes off from Skelton's *Calliope* and has much good to say about
"old John" throughout. Alone among first-rate scholars and
critics, C. S. Lewis, in his comprehensive *English Literature in
the Sixteenth Century* (1954), views Skelton with less than enthusiasm. W. H. Auden, E. M. Forster, and John Holloway,
among others, have paid public tribute to him in recent years;
and monographs elucidating various aspects of his work and art
now appear in the publishing lists. A final mark of triumph for
Skelton is the new critical edition of his works being prepared
by one of his most astute and perceptive critics, Robert Kinsman.

"Strong, rough Skelton!" wrote Mrs. Browning. "The man is
very strong—he triumphs, foams, is rabid, in the sense of
strength." The triumph, the strength, the wit, the humor—these
are his most enduring qualities today. But let the old laureate
speak for himself—in the Latin hexameters he prefaced to the
apologia pro sua vita, the *Garland of Laurel.* "While the stars
shine with alternate day," he begins sweepingly and with no
false modesty (in Henderson's translation), "and while the seas
swell, these our laurels shall be green; our illustrious name shall
be translated to the sky, and everywhere shall Skelton be re-
nowned as another Adonis."

Notes and References

Chapter One

1. Older sources speak of Cumberland or Norfolk as likely birthplaces for Skelton: see, for example, Thomas Fuller, *History of the Worthies of England* (London, 1662), I, 221, and II, 257, and Anthony à Wood, *Athenae Oxonienses* (London, 1691), I, 20–21. Latest research on the subject, however, makes a strong case for Yorkshire, where there are six towns by this name, and an even greater number with Skelton as the second word in the name of the town: see Maurice Pollet, *John Skelton* (Paris, 1962), pp. 24–28.

It is worth pointing out that to the end of his life Skelton seems to have retained a great dislike for the neighboring Scots, typical of one who lived in the North.

2. See *A Replycacion,* in *The Poetical Works of John Skelton,* ed. Alexander Dyce (London, 1843), I, 207: "Cantabrigia Skeltonidi laureato primam mammam eruditionis pientissime propinavit." All quotations from Skelton are taken from the Dyce edition.

3. See Thomas Alfred Walker, *A Biographical Register of Peterhouse Men,* Part I, 1284–1574 (Cambridge, 1927), p. 101; John Venn and J. A. Venn, *Alumni cantabrigienses* (Cambridge, 1922–44), IV, 82; and *Grace Book A,* ed. Stanley M. Leathes (Cambridge, 1897), p. 134. For a handy discussion of various Cambridge Skeltons, see William Nelson, *John Skelton, Laureate* (New York, 1939), pp. 60–61.

4. *Caxton's Eneydos,* 1490, ed. W. T. Culley and F. J. Furnivall (London, 1890), p. 3.

5. See *Grace Book B,* Part I, ed. Mary Bateson (Cambridge, 1903), p. 54: "Conceditur Johanni Skelton poete in partibus transmarinis atque oxonie laurea ornato ut aput [sic] nos eadem decoraretur."

6. The *Tales* are printed in Dyce's edition of Skelton: see I, lvii.

7. *Ibid.,* I, lviii. Whether true or not, this story gives us such insight into Skelton's sharp wit and pungent humor that I cannot resist quoting more of it:

Syr, sayde the man, I will put you a question: you do know wel that after Christ dyd rise from death to life, it was xl. days after ere he

dyd ascend into heauen, an hee was but certaine times wyth hys dis-
cyples, and when that he did appeare to them, hee dyd neuer tary
longe amongest them, but sodainely vanished from them; I wold
fayne know (saith the man to Skelton) where Chryste was all these
xl. days. Where hee was, saythe Skelton, God knoweth; he was verye
busye in the woods among hys labourers, that dyd make fagottes to
burn heretickes, & such as thou art the whych doest aske such diffuse
questions. . . .

8. For a discussion of the meaning of the laureation, see Nelson,
pp. 40 ff. See also F. M. Salter and H. L. R. Edwards, ed. *The Bibliotheca Historica of Diodorus Siculus, Translated by John Skelton*
(EETS, London, 1956–57), II, xxxiv. There are only three recorded
grants of the laurel in English universities—to Skelton, Bulman, and
Whittington. Salter points out that for a brief period, the laurel was a
badge of a degree in rhetoric, as the rod and birch were insignia of a
master of grammar. In all cases the rhetorician would have studied
grammar, and his was the higher degree.

9. For Skelton's private calendar, see Nelson, pp. 62, 173–74.

10. Dyce, I, 128. Nelson, p. 62, was the first to remark upon the
obvious detachment with which Skelton refers to Oxford: "their senate" seems to place him outside rather than among those closely attached to Oxford. And although the University Senate is the governing
body at Cambridge, this is not true of Oxford. H. L. R. Edwards, *Skelton: The Life and Times of an Early Tudor Poet* (London, 1949), pp.
36–38, argues for the possibility that King Henry himself awarded the
laurel to Skelton during the summer of 1488 when in the neighborhood
of Oxford.

11. Dyce, I, 197.

12. See Nelson, pp. 4 ff., for an excellent discussion of the humanists
at the court of Henry VII.

13. See the account of the insurrection in Dyce, II, 89.

14. *Caxton's Eneydos*, p. 4.

15. Dyce, I, 409, 420.

16. For an account of the embassy and the response of Henry's humanists to Gaguin's invective, see James Gairdner, *Henry the Seventh*
(London, 1920), pp. 75 ff. See also Nelson, pp. 25 ff.

Philip Henderson, ed. *The Complete Poems of John Skelton* (London and Toronto, 1931), p. 143, prints a few lines of invective which
Brie discovered among MSS at Trinity College, Cambridge, and
printed in his *Skelton-Studien* (1907) as the lost poem against Gaguin.
In Henderson's 2nd ed. of Skelton's works (1948), the verses do not
appear.

17. Dyce, I, xvi–xix, reprints the entire poem, ending, "Quæ Whitin-

tonus canit ad laudes tibi, Schelton, / Anglorum vatum gloria, sume libens." The poem is from the *Opusculum Roberti Whittintoni*, printed by Wynken de Worde in 1519. Dyce notes (p. xv) that there is no mention of Skelton in the Louvain registers.

18. See Nelson, p. 63, citing H. de Jongh, *L'Ancienne faculté de théologie de Louvain* (1911).

19. Edwards, p. 46, makes this conjecture.

20. See note 5.

21. See the statement of Lord Herbert of Cherbury, *The Life and Reign of King Henry the Eighth* (London, 1672), p. 2: "His education was accurate, being destined (as a credible Author affirms) to the Archbishoprick of *Canterbury*, during the life of his elder brother Prince *Arthur;* that prudent King his father chusing this as the most cheap and glorious way of bestowing a younger son. . . ." A marginal note cites the authority: Concil. Trid. 1. I. That is, Paolo Sarpi's *History of the Council of Trent.*

22. See C. A. Halstead, *Life of Margaret Beaufort* (London, 1839), pp. 196–97.

23. Long thought lost (see Dyce, I, xxi, when he speaks of Tanner's having seen the poem in the MS Library of Lincoln Cathedral), these verses have been printed from a MS in the British Museum by F. M. Salter, "Skelton's *Speculum Principis*," *Speculum*, IX (1934), 36–37. For cogent argument that the verses were indeed written for Henry's creation, see Nelson, pp. 73–74.

24. Dyce, I, 129.

25. John Bale, *Index Britanniae Scriptorum*, ed. Reginald Lane Poole and Mary Bateson (Oxford, 1902), p. 252, citing William Horman: "Ionnes Skelton, pastor ecclesie de Dysse in Nordouolgia, Oxoniij poeta laureatus, vates ac preceptor regius erat."

26. *Speculum*, IX, 28 ff.

27. *Ibid.*, p. 32. Professor Salter also notes that Skelton's lost poem in honor of "Prince Arthur's Creacyoun" might have been written either in 1489, when Arthur was created Knight of the Bath, or in 1491, when he was made Knight of the Garter (in addition to his creation Prince of Wales, generally thought to have been the occasion for the poem). Salter, in fact, believed that the poem was written in 1489 when Skelton had charge of Arthur's education (see pp. 32–33). For Caxton's remarks, see *Eneydos*, p. 4.

28. See the introduction by Salter and Edwards, *Diodorus Siculus*, I, x.

29. Caxton's *Eneydos*, p. 4. And see the often quoted remarks of Raphael Holinshed in his *Chronicles* (London, repr. of 1808), III, 557, that Henry exercised himself daily in "singing, dansing, . . . plaieng at the recorders, flute, virginals, in setting of songs, and making of

ballads; he did set two full masses, euerie of them fiue parts, which were
soong oftentimes in his chappell, and afterwards in diuers other places."
  30. See *Grace Book B*, I, 92:

  Item die Mercurii pro Jantaculo cum Magistro Skelton quia
  fuit cum episcopo Sarum   vd
  Item die saboti pro Jantaculo cum Magistro Skelton apud
  Symsons   iiijd

For a discussion of this case, see Edwards, pp. 48–50.
  31. Dyce, I, 410. See *ibid.*, II, 328, for Caxton and Pynson. Lydgate's *Pilgrimage of the Life of Man* has been published by the EETS.
None of these versions of the *Pélerinage* has been related to Skelton,
however. For a handy listing of the "lost" works from Skelton's *Garland*, see L. J. Lloyd, *John Skelton, A Sketch of his Life and Writings*
(Oxford, 1938), pp. 142–44.
  32. Dyce, I, 416.
  33. See Edwards, p. 288, quoting from an unpublished MS in the
Public Record Office, E 101, 414–16.
  34. Records of Oxford degrees for these years are missing, but we
know of the poet's higher degree at Oxford because of a clear statement in a Cambridge grace of 1504/5 where, under "Masters of Arts,"
Skelton was given the same status that he enjoyed at Oxford. See
Grace Book Gamma, ed. William George Searle (Cambridge, 1908),
p. 37. In the biography of Skelton by Edward Braynewode, printed by
Bale in his *Index* (253), the poet is called "theologię professor." He
is called "doctor Skelton" in Rowley's play of 1605: see p. 126 below.
  35. See Dyce, I, xx–xxi, for the entries from Register *Hill*, 1489–
1505, Diocese of London, recording Skelton's ordinations. Dates are
March 31, April 14, and June 9.
  36. See George Cavendish, *The Life and Death of Cardinal Wolsey*,
ed. Richard S. Sylvester (EETS, London, New York, Toronto, 1959),
p. 193.
  37. Peter Green, *John Skelton* (London, 1960), p. 14.
  38. PRO MS E. 101. 414–16:

  Item for offring opon Sonday   vj s   viij d (Nov 11)
  Item for offring at master Skelton masse   xx s (Nov 16)

Nelson, p. 71, and Edwards, p. 288, cite these records.
  39. See Nelson, pp. 80 ff. and Edwards, p. 264, note 47, for conclusions about servants and salary by analogy with the remuneration of
other royal schoolmasters.
  40. See P. S. Allen, *Opus Epistolarum Erasmi* (Oxonii, 1906–58),

I, 6 (letter 1, 1523—that is, the letter was written twenty-five years after the event described in it). Dyce, I, xxiv–xxv, also cites the Latin original. For an English translation, see Francis Morgan Nichols, *The Epistles of Erasmus* (London, 1901), pp. 201–2:

> I was staying at lord Mountjoy's country house when Thomas More came to see me, and took me out with him for a walk as far as the next village, where all the king's children, except prince Arthur, who was then the eldest son, were being educated. When we came into the hall, the attendants not only of the palace but also of Mount-joy's household were all assembled. In the midst stood prince Henry, then nine years old, and having already something of royalty in his demeanour, in which there was a certain dignity combined with singular courtesy. On his right was Margaret, about eleven years of age, afterwards married to James, king of Scots; and on his left played Mary, a child of four. Edmund was an infant in arms. More, with his companion Arnold, after paying his respects to the boy Henry, the same that is now king of England, presented him with some writing. For my part, not having expected anything of the sort, I had nothing to offer, but promised that on another occasion I would in some way declare my duty towards him. Meantime I was angry with More for not having warned me, especially as the boy sent me a little note, while we were at dinner, to challenge something from my pen. I went home, and in the Muses' spite, from whom I had been so long divorced, finished the poem within three days.

The poem (*Prosopopœia Britanniæ*) was printed in 1500, Nichols states, with the *Adages*. Allen, I, 6, note 5, points out that two of the ages are wrong by one year: Henry was born June 2, 1491; Margaret, November 29, 1489. Mary was born March 18, 1495; Edmund, February 21, 1498.

41. See Allen, *Epistolae Erasmi*, I, 241 (letter 104, 1499): "et domi haberes Skeltonum, vnum Britannicarum litterarum lumen ac decus, qui tua studia possit non solum accendere sed etiam consummare." Bale includes this statement in his notice of Skelton in the *Index:* see p. 252. Erasmus' flowery phrase "Britannicarum litterarum lumen ac decus" has been quoted many times since.

Nichols translates only part of letter 104, omitting this part. For an English translation, see Edwards, p. 68. Edwards' documentation of these references is confused and difficult to follow.

42. See Dyce, I, xxiii for the original: "Jam puer Henricus, genitoris nomine lætus, / *Monstrante fonteis vate Skeltono sacros,* / Palladias teneris meditatur ab unguibus arteis." Nelson, p. 72, gives an English translation.

43. Edwards, pp. 289–90, quotes the original from MS Egerton 1651. For a translation, see Preserved Smith, *Erasmus* (New York, 1923), p. 62.

44. See *Grace Book B*, I, 148–49 (1501, Hilary term—between January 11 and March 24:

Item die Mercurii apud Westmonasterium in iantaculo nostro   ijd
Item eodem die pro cena nostra et Magistri skelton   vjd
Item eodem die [Martis] pro cena nostra et magistro skelton   vjd
Item eodem die [marcurii] pro cena cum Magistro skelton in hospicio   vjd
Item [die Jouis] in camera pro focali et potu cum Magistro skelton   ijd

45. Nelson, p. 69. See the last item above.

46. See *ibid.*, p. 242, for the notice from the Act Book of the Court of Requests, PRO. And see *ibid.*, pp. 76–78, for a discussion of the case.

47. See Salter, *Speculum*, IX, 29, for dating of the treatise. Salter believed that Skelton had been Arthur's tutor as well as Henry's, and that the treatise was perhaps inspired by the impending separation of tutor and older pupil—who was to marry Catherine of Aragon in a few months' time: see pp. 29–33.

48. See Nelson, p. 74, and Edwards, p. 289, quoting from PRO MS E 101. 415–3: "Item to the duc of yorks scolemaster xl s." Nelson also calls attention to the fact (p. 75) that "Prince Arthur's schoolmaster, a nameless Scot, received twenty shillings from Queen Elizabeth 'at his departing'" and that perhaps such parting gifts were customary. For the original, see Nicholas Harris Nicolas, *Privy Purse Expenses of Elizabeth of York* (London, 1830), p. 28 (July, 1502): "Item the same day to the said Lady Bray for money by hur geven to a Scottisheman scole maister to the prince at his departing by the Quenes commaundement   xx s."

49. See *Grace Book Gamma* (1504/5) p. 37, where Hoone is among the Masters of Arts (along with Skelton) incorporated from Oxford; here he is called "institutor domini principis." On p. 121 (1514/5) it is recorded that he commenced Bachelor of Theology, at which time he was called "royal chaplain" ("regius capellanus").

50. Dyce, I, xxvi, mentions the notice. Nelson, pp. 242–43, cites it in full from the PRO Act Book. Edwards, pp. 78–79, translates it. Apparently the Prior of St. Bartholomew's and others had borrowed a considerable sum of money from Sir Reginald Bray, royal councillor, and others, and Skelton stood surety for them. When the money was not paid on time, Skelton had to appear before the court. Edwards makes out a strong case for the phrase "carceribus genitoris domini regis" to

mean "the prison of the king's mother" and not "the prison of the king's jailor," as has long been thought. If this interpretation is correct, it further connects the poet—if indeed the defendant is the poet—with the Lady Margaret's household.

51. Edwards, p. 291, quotes the record discovered by Nelson in a Court register at Norwich.

52. *Ibid.*, pp. 85–86.

53. See *Grace Book Gamma* (1504/5), p. 37: "Item conceditur Johanni Skelton poete laureato quod possit stare eodem gradu hic quo stetit Oxoniis et quod possit vti habitu sibi concesso a principe." This certainly gives the lie to the old belief that Skelton retired in disgrace to Norfolk: the university would never have dared honor an exile from court in such a way.

54. See *ibid.*, pp. 37–38, for the graces of these men. And see Nan C. Carpenter, *Music in the Medieval and Renaissance Universities* (Norman, 1958), pp. 201 ff., for musical customs connected with the taking of degrees at Cambridge.

55. For the same reason, rare graduates in music were allowed special dispensation with regard to their attire—sometimes wearing the robes of the medical faculty. See *ibid.*, pp. 199–200, 205–7, for special concessions with regard to the wearing of gowns.

56. See the statement following the poem on Adam Uddersall, Dyce, I, 173: "*Finis, &c. Apud Trumpinton scriptum per Curatum ejusdem, quinto die Januarii Anno Domini, secundum computat. Angliae, MDVII.*" There are many references to the Vicar (or Rector) of Trumpington throughout *Grace Book Beta*, I, usually to his being paid for writing letters for the university ("pro scriptura diuersarum literarum"). I cannot find that he is anywhere identified.

At least one older source identifies the poet himself with the Vicar of Trumpington: see Thomas Alfred Walker, *A Biographical Register of Peterhouse Men*, Part I, 1284–1574 (Cambridge, 1927), who states (p. 101), that Skelton's literary services were "much in request for correspondence between the University and the Lady Margaret." The reference to John Skelton is a note following the item on William Skelton —"? B. A. 1478/9"—which is obviously the source of the conjecture (found in most of the Skelton biographies) that the poet may have taken a degree at Peterhouse in 1478/9.

A "Tetrastichon Skelton. Laureati Ad Magistrum Rukshaw, Sacræ Theologiæ Egregium Professorem" (Dyce, I, 14) connects Skelton with a distinguished Fellow of Peterhouse, William Ruckshaw. The four lines ask the doctor to accept some poems ("*Accipe nunc demum, doctor celeberrime Rukshaw, / Carmina, de calamo quæ cecidere meo . . .*"), and since this was printed immediately following the elegy on the Earl of Northumberland in Marshe's edition of 1568, some scholars have thought the elegy was addressed to Ruckshaw. Cf., for example, Walker, *Register of Peterhouse Men,* I, 57; "When Henry, Earl of Northumberland, was killed in a popular tumult in 1489 John Skelton, the poet, composed a dirge and addressed it to Rowkeshawe, who was evidently in the Earl's service." It is true that Ruckshaw was given his two main benefices by the Earl: see Edwards, p. 32.

57. *Skelton,* p. 12.

58. Although Skelton's learned editor, the Reverend Mr. Dyce, put no stock whatever in the truth of these anecdotes, calling them a "tissue of extravagant figments which was put together for the amusement of the vulgar" (I, xxx), later critics have taken a different view. See, for example, Nelson, pp. 109–10. The *Tales* are reprinted in Dyce, I, lvii–lxxiii.

It is interesting to record that "the jestes of Skelton" were found in an inventory of possessions of Thomas Cromwell, 1534, according to no. 923, p. 341, *Letters and Papers of the Reign of Henry VIII,* VII, ed. James Gairdner (London, 1883).

59. Tale vi, Dyce, I, lx–lxi:

Skelton dyd keepe a musket at Dys, vpon the which he was com-playned on to the bishop of Norwych. The byshoppe sent for Skel-ton. Skelton dyd take two capons, to geue theym for a presente to the byshop. . . . The bishop sayd, A hoare head! I will none of thy capons: thou keepest vnhappy rule in thy house, for the wyche thou shalt be punished. . . . The byshop sent after Skelton to come agayne. Skelton sayde, What, shal I come agayne to speake wythe a madde man? At last hee retourned to the byshop, whyche sayde to hym, I would, sayd the byshop, that you shoulde not lyue suche a sclaunderouse lyfe, that all your parisshe shoulde not wonder & complaine on you as they dooe; I pray you amende, and hereafter lyue honestlye, that I heare no more suche woordes of you; and if you wyll tarye dynner, you shall be welcome; and I thanke you, sayde the byshoppe, for your capons. Skelton sayde, My lord, my capons haue proper names; the one is named Alpha, the other is named Omega: my lorde, sayd Skelton, this capon is named Alpha, thys is the fyrst capon that I dyd euer geue to you; and this capon is named Omega, and this is the last capon that euer I will giue you: & so fare you well, sayd Skelton.

60. Tale vii, *ibid.,* I, lxi:

Skelton the nexte Sondaye after wente into the pulpet to prech, and sayde . . . You haue complayned of mee to the bysop that I doo keepe a fayre wench in my house. . . . I am a man as you be . . .

and I haue a faire wenche, of the whyche I haue begotten a fayre
boye, as I doe thinke, and as you all shall see. Thou wyfe, sayde
Skelton, that hast my childe, be not afraid; bring me hither my
childe to me: the whyche was doone. And he, shewynge his childe
naked to all the parishe, sayde, How saye you, neibours all? is not
this child as fayre as is the beste of all yours? It hathe nose, eyes,
handes, and feete, as well as any of your: it is not lyke a pygge,
nor a calfe, nor like no foule nor no monstruous beast. If I had,
Sayde Skelton, broughte forth thys chylde without armes or legges,
or that it wer deformed, being a monstruous thyng, I woulde neuer
haue blamed you to haue complayned to the bishop of me; but to
complain without a cause, I say, as I said before . . . you be, and
haue be, & wyll and shall be knaues, to complayne of me wythout a
cause resonable. . . .

61. One can cause much interesting speculation at the Huntington
lunch table by asking scholars who was buried in Wolsey's tomb. After
going through many vicissitudes, Wolsey's splendid cenotaph finally
came to rest in St. Paul's where it was used to cover the body of Lord
Nelson. See Edwards, p. 244.

62. Bale, *Index*, p. 253: "Cum quibusdam mendicantium fratrum
blateronibus, precipue Dominicanis, continuum gerebat bellum. Sub
pseudoepiscopo Nordouicensi Ricardo [Richard Nikke, Nix, Nick],
mulierem quam secreto desponsauerat, vt Antichristi vitaret obprobria,
sub concubine titulo custodiebat, quam tamen in mortis articulo con-
fitebatur se prolegitima semper tenuisse coniuge." This was the basis
of Fuller's account of Skelton in his *Worthies* of 1622. See Chapter 3
below.

63. See *Letters and Papers, Foreign and Domestic, of the Reign of
Henry VIII*, ed. J. S. Brewer, II, Part II (London, 1864), 1518. The
preceding page (1517) contains a detailed description of "the King's
revel stuff"—gorgeous costumes, ornaments, hats, etc., "in the charge
of John Farlyon, lately deceased, and now committed to one Brigges,
appointed in his place."
See Dyce, I, viii–ix, for a copy of the poem. (Note that there are
two sets of pages viii–ix. The poem is found in the first set.)

64. Although Edwards, p. 126, implies that this was the first use of
the image of the two roses—"an image from which was to spring the
entire Tudor Myth"—actually Skelton's poem was antedated by a song
found in the Fayrfax MS, "I love, I love, and whom love ye?" (Date
of the MS is before 1500.) The poem not only celebrates the union of
the two houses, but refers to the birth of a son to Henry VII and Elizabeth of York in stanzas 6, 8, 9. See stanza 8:

'I love the rose, both red and white.'
'Is that your pure perfytt appetite?'
'To here talke of them is my delite.
Joyed may we be
Our prince to see, and rosys thre.'

For the entire poem, see John Stevens, *Music and Poetry in the Early Tudor Court* (London, 1961), pp. 364–65.

65. See Salter, *Speculum*, IX, 37, for a copy of the verses.

66. Edwards, p. 298, prints the pardon from the PRO Supplementary Patent Rolls. See the general pardon orders in *Letters and Papers*, ed. J. S. Brewer, I (London, 1862), 2, 3.

67. Nelson, p. 243, cites the records of this case from the Act Book of the Consistory Court, preserved at Norwich Cathedral.

68. For the facts of this case, see *ibid.*, p. 114. For information about Wolsey and the Redgrave living, see A. F. Pollard, *Wolsey* (London, New York, Toronto, 1929), p. 13n.

69. Nelson, p. 118, gives the names of Skelton's substitutes.

70. See *ibid.*, 118, for items comprised in the dinner:

Item ij playce	vij d
Item ij copull soliz	vj d
Item ij Congger snekes	xiiij d
Item a syd saltffishe	ij d
Item ij disches buter	ij d

71. See Salter, *Speculum*, IX, 29. Edwards believes the volume was a gift for New Year's, 1511, and that the *Chronique* was a similar gift for the same time, 1512: see pp. 129–32. For the Latin *Complaint*, see *Speculum*, IX, 37. Edwards (p. 130) translates the Latin, although his Latin version (p. 310) is not quite identical with Salter's, which I follow here. Nelson (p. 117) also has an English translation of most of the *Complaint*.

72. See Pollard, *Wolsey*, pp. 13 ff.

73. See Nelson, pp. 116–18, for a facsimile of Skelton's dedication to the King from a MS in Corpus Christi College, Cambridge. Nelson believes that the *Chronique* was part of Skelton's coronation gift. Edwards (p. 132) translates the first few lines of the Latin dedication (p. 310).

74. See H. L. R. Edwards, "The Dating of Skelton's Later Poems," *PMLA*, LIII (1938), 601–3, for clarification with regard to the date of Skelton's assumption of the title *orator regius*. First of all, Edwards demonstrates that the numeral 24 at the end of the dedication of the

Chronique (see facsimile, Nelson, p. 174)—the 24th year of Skelton's private calendar—fixes the presentation of the French poem between October 30, 1511, and November 17, 1512. This confirms, Edwards continues, the statement of du Resnel that Skelton's patent dated from the fifth year of Henry's reign—1512 or 1513. There is no mention of the oratorship in any poem written before April, 1512, when Henry's fifth year began; there is prolific mention of it in poems written after this time. Wolsey's engineering of the war against France in 1512 is the occasion, Edwards thinks, of Skelton's triple warning in his *Complaint* following the *Speculum principis* to beware of Ishmael (Wolsey). All these facts and others lead Edwards to conclude that Skelton was appointed royal orator in May, 1512.

For the statement of du Resnel ("la patente qui declare Skelton poète laureat d'Henry viii. est datée de la cinquième année de son règne, ce qui tombe en 1512 ou 1513"), see Dyce, I, xv. The letters patent are no longer in existence.

Pollet, *Skelton,* pp. 87–88, dates the royal oratorship 1513, instead of 1512, on the basis of the poem *Against Venomous Tongues,* which has the superscription *Orator regius tertius,* that is, third year as royal orator, and which contains a reference to the tournament of Tottenham, which took place on May 4, 1516.

75. See Bale, *Index,* p. 253: "Ob literas in Cardinalem Wolsium inuectivas, ad Westmonasteriense asylum confugere pro vita seruanda coactus fuit, vbi tamen sub Islepo abbate fauorem inuenit."

76. See William Camden, *Reges, Reginae, Nobiles, et Alii in Ecclesia Collegiata B. Petri Westmonasterij Sepulti* (Londini, 1603), D *verso,* where above Skelton's verses are the words "In tabula pensili" —that is, the epitaph was mounted on a panel and hung up. The verses to Henry VII follow the words "In altera tabula pensili"—hanging on another panel (D2 *verso*)—and the epitaph for the Lady Margaret follows "In tabula pensili" (D3 *verso*). Since Camden states on the title page that he has brought his work up to the year 1603 ("Vsque ad annum reparatæ Salutis 1603")—up to 1606, he states in the second edition—the epitaphs must have actually been hanging near the tombs at that time. Printed in full by Camden, these verses, in fact, were used as a source by Dyce in his edition of Skelton's poems: see I, 178n, 195n. For the epitaphs, see Dyce, I, 178–81 and 195–96.

77. See John Weever, *Ancient Fvnerall Monvments within the Vnited Monarchie of Great Britaine, Ireland, and the Islands adiacent* . . . (London, 1631), p. 476. Weever continues, "I will take onely the shortest of his Epitaphs or Eulogiums, and most to the purpose," and cites eight lines of Latin verse beginning, "*Septimus hic situs est Henricus, gloria Regum,*" which is included but not ascribed to Skel-

ton in Camden's *Reges, Reginae,* and which Dyce did not see fit to include in his edition (see his note, II, 214).

78. See A. F. Pollard, *Henry VIII* (London, Paris, New York, 1902), pp. 47–50, and Pollard, *Wolsey,* pp. 18–19. For a colorful contemporary account of Henry's campaign in France, see Edward Hall, *The Vnion of the Two Noble and Illustre Famelies of Lancastre & Yorke* . . . (London, 1548), "The triumphaunt reigne of Kyng Henry the .VIII."

79. This *Chorus* and the next are found in Dyce, I, 190–91.

80. See *A Ballade of the Scottysshe Kynge,* ed. John Ashton (London, 1882), p. 11.

81. Dyce, I, 182–89.

82. Nelson, pp. 126–29, makes a strong case for Skelton's presence in France. Edwards, however, pp. 136–41, takes the opposite view—that Skelton stayed at home, where he received news of the French victory through the Queen, and that he wrote his hasty ballad for the Queen—left to rule the country while Henry was abroad—on the basis of the fact that in two early editions of the poem Skelton signs himself "*Reginę orator,*" "orator of the Queen." Dyce, I, 190, noticed this signature but assumed that it was a misprint.

83. See *Letters and Papers,* I, 634, no. 4314. Many items from the year 1513, in fact, record in specific detail the careful preparations—made by the King's Almoner in many instances—for the sortie into France, and make fascinating reading.

84. See Holinshed, *Chronicles,* III, 588, quoting Hall. Nelson, p. 128, notes the mistake in dating (25 and 26 September should be 21 and 22 September).

85. For the facts about Garnesche and the dating of the poem, see Dyce, I, xxx–xxxiv; the article in the *DNB;* and Helen Stearnes Sale, "John Skelton and Christopher Garnesche," *Modern Language Notes,* XLII (1928), 518–23. See Edwards, pp. 146 ff., for a summary of information about Garnesche.

Several references to him appear in *Letters and Papers,* I (see the index). According to these records, his annuity of ten pounds in 1509 was doubled the next year, and in later years he was given several manors and estates confiscated by the Crown. Hall's *Chronicle,* fol. xlviij (1548 ed.) tells the most famous story about Garnesche—how he rescued the Princess Mary from possible shipwreck as she was landing in France. Garnesche outlived Skelton, dying an exile in France in 1534. In 1520 he had a share in organizing the Field of the Cloth of Gold.

86. Pollard, *Wolsey,* pp. 20–21.

87. See Nelson, p. 120, and Edwards, p. 180. Edwards, pp. 298–299, prints the document.

88. See Dyce, I, 175–76. For all the facts about Bedell, see Edwards, pp. 155–58. Edwards attempts a translation of part of the epitaph, p. 157.
89. Pollard, *Wolsey*, pp. 55–58.
90. *Ibid.*, pp. 123 ff., and see the introduction by J. S. Brewer, *Letters and Papers*, III.
91. Braynewode's statement in Bale's *Index* (p. 253) has already been cited: see note 75 above. See also Tale xiv of the *Merie Tales*, Dyce, I, lxxii: How Skelton was in prison at the commaundement of the cardinall:

On a tyme Skelton did meete with certain frendes of hys at Charyng crosse, after that hee was in prison at my lord cardynals commaundement: & his frende sayd, I am glad you bee abrode amonge your frendes, for you haue ben long pent in. Skelton sayd, By the masse, I am glad I am out indeede, for I haue ben pent in, like a roche or fissh, at Westminster in prison. The cardinal, hearing of those words, sent for him agayne. Skelton kneling of hys knees before hym, after long communication to Skelton had. Skelton desyred the cardinall to graunte hym a boun. Thou shalt have none, sayd the cardynall. Thassistence desirid that he might haue it graunted, for they thought it should be some merye pastime that he wyll shewe your grace. Say on, thou hore head, sayd the cardynall to Skelton. I pray your grace to let me lye doune and wallow, for I can kneele no longer.

92. The envoy was not published in Fawkes's edition of the *Garland of Laurel* of 1523, but was published by Marshe in the collected edition of the poems, 1568. See Dyce, I, 424.
93. Hall, edition of 1548.
94. See the fascinating account of Buckingham's trial and execution in Brewer's introduction, *Letters and Papers*, III, cx ff.
95. I am indebted for this observation to my Huntington colleague, Dr. A. L. Rowse.
96. See William Smith, ed. *Old Yorkshire* (London, 1881), p. 104, and Joseph E. Morris, *The North Riding of Yorkshire* (3rd ed., London, 1931), p. 345. Remains of Sheriff-Hutton Castle are still standing, on a little hill, and a formidable sight they are when viewed from a distance. Not far away is a village called Skelton. I am deeply indebted to my good friend, the Hon. Mary Lawson-Tancred, for much pleasant Yorkshire hospitality, with excursions to Sheriff-Hutton and other interesting spots.
97. Dyce, I, 424.

98. *Ibid.*, II, 83–84. For a discussion of the promise, see Nelson, p. 203.

99. Dyce, I, 206. These Latin dedications and envoys are translated in the Henderson edition of Skelton's poems.

100. Records of the trial appear in *Letters and Papers*, IV (ii), no. 4242. For easy reference, see Edwards, p. 303. It was Edwards who discovered Skelton's name here: see his article, *PMLA*, LIII, 610. A fuller is one whose work is to *full*—or beat—cloth to clean or thicken it.

101. See Bale, *Index*, p. 253: "Mortuus tandem, in D. Margarete templo ante summum altare conditus est, cum hac scriptione alabastrica. Ioannes Skeltonus vates pierius hic situs est. Animam egit xxj. die Junij, A.D. 1529."

102. These records are printed by Nelson, p. 219, and Edwards, p. 304:

Item of Master skelton for iiij tapers	ijs	viijd
Item of hym for iiij torches	iiijs	
Item of M Iohn skelton for knyll and peales	vjs	viijd
Item paid to or lady brotherhed for M skelton		xxd
Item paid for Ringyng of his knyll and peales		xijd

For an explanation of the Brotherhood, see Edwards, p. 254.

103. See Nelson, p. 220, for the record from the Norwich Institution Book, XVII.

104. See *ibid.*, p. 220, and Edwards, p. 304, where the entire record is printed.

Chapter Two

1. Dyce, I, 409, 410, 420–21.

2. See the splendid introduction by F. M. Salter and H. L. R. Edwards, *The Bibliotheca Historica of Diodorus Siculus*, trans. John Skelton (EETS, London, New York, Toronto, 1956–57), II, xxii–xxiii.

3. *Ibid.*, II, xlii. For an exceedingly clear analysis of Skelton's rhetorical style, see "Skelton and Rhetoric," *ibid.*, II, xxxiv–xlvii.

4. See, for example, L. J. Lloyd, *John Skelton* (Oxford, 1938), p. 141.

5. Salter and Edwards, *Diodorus Siculus*, I, 24–25. Throughout this edition, notes show how Skelton amplified the Latin he was translating.

6. *Ibid.*, I, 357–60.

7. See *ibid.*, I, xiv, for dating of the Corpus Christi College MS containing Skelton's translation.

8. Dyce, I, 1–5.

9. *Ibid.*, I, 408. This may have been some version of Caxton's translation from the French: *A lityll treatise . . . spekyng of the arte and crafte to knowe well to dye* (1490). Or it may have been a translation of a Latin *art of dying.*

10. Deschamps and Villon also have such lists. See Leonard P. Kurtz, *The Dance of Death and the Macabre Spirit in European Literature* (New York, 1934), pp. 11–12. See also the discussion of the *Vade Mori* poems (pp. 16–17), in which each strophe begins and ends with the phrase "Je vais mourir." Skelton's elegy seems to echo this trend also.

11. For an excellent account of the beginnings and development of the idea of the dance of death in various media, see James M. Clark, *The Dance of Death in the Middle Ages and Renaissance* (Glasgow, 1950). Skelton would surely have known Lydgate's famous translation of the French *danse macabre* from the Church of the Holy Innocents at Paris, where paintings of the dance were done in 1424. According to John Stow, *A Survey of London* (London, 1598), p. 264, the pictures were reproduced in St. Paul's Cathedral during the reign of Henry VI. (The paintings have long since disappeared.) For an account of the dance of death in literature, see the introduction to John Lydgate's poem by Florence Warren and Beatrice White, *The Dance of Death* (EETS, London, 1931). In none of these sources is there mention of John Skelton.

12. For a handy listing of these (although with a minimum of explanation), see Charles Sears Baldwin, *Medieval Rhetoric and Poetic* (New York, 1928), pp. 304–5.

13. See *The Poems of William Dunbar*, ed. David Laing (Edinburgh, 1834), I, 249–50. This, too, must have owed something to St. Bernard, in idea and in the singling out of Hector, Hercules, Achilles, Samson, Alexander, David, and Absalom. For other poems with Latin refrains, see, e.g., I, 211, 236, 247, etc.

14. Dyce, I, 6–14. For circumstances of the Earl's death, see Dyce, II, 89. Dyce, II, 91, reminds us that the fifth earl was only eleven years old at his father's death.

It has been suggested by Salter and Edwards (*Diodorus Siculus*, II, xxxviii) that the elegy is closely modeled on that of Geoffrey de Vinsauf for Richard I, which illustrates the use of *exclamatio*, and that Skelton's poem is thus quite conventional. It is true that several of Skelton's apostrophes are similar to those of Geoffrey—e.g., both apostrophize the day of the murder, as Salter and Edwards point out ("O *Veneris* lacrimosa dies! O! Sydus amarum! / Illa die tua nox fuit, et *Venus* illa venenum," moans Geoffrey. And Skelton says, "O dolorous tewisday, dedicate to thy name"). But there is nothing in Skelton's poem to equal Geoffrey's line "O! dolor! o! plusquam dolor!" and as a matter of fact, Skelton is halfway through his poem before he introduces the examples of *exclamatio* to which Salter and Edwards refer. Geoffrey's poem, too, ends on an entirely different note: "Sed in hac Re scire dedisti, / Quam brevis est risus, quam longa est Lachryma mundi." See Geoffrey's *Lamentatio de morte Regis Ricardi* found at the end of *Benedicti Abbatis Petroburgensis de Vita et Gestis Henrici II. & Ricardi I* (Oxonii, 1735), II, 748–50.

There is similarity between Skelton's elegy and that of Dunbar on the death of Bernard Stewart: see Laing, *Poems of Dunbar*, I, 133–34. But since the latter did not die until 1508, the influence, if any, must have been in the opposite direction.

15. Dyce, I, 22–27.

16. Salter and Edwards, *Diodorus Siculus*, II, xxxvii, call this poem "an ecphrasis in the aureate manner of Lydgate." For the conventional description known as *ecphrasis*, see Baldwin, *Medieval Rhetoric*, pp. 17–20.

17. Dyce, I, 20–21. For identification of the Key in Thames Street, see Edwards, p. 53.

18. Dyce, I, 411. Henderson, p. 27, includes another short poem "To Mistress Anne" ("Mistress Anne, / I am your man") sometimes attributed to Skelton.

19. See Nan C. Carpenter, *Rabelais and Music* (Chapel Hill, 1954), p. 24. In the play *Hyckescorner*, printed by Wynken de Worde c. 1512 (fac. ed. London, 1908) Freewill asks, "Good syr why do men ete mustarde with befe?" and Perseverance answers, "Peas man thou talkest lewdly" (fol. C i).

20. Dyce, I, 409–10.

21. *Ibid.*, I, 28–29. Sir John Hawkins, *A General History of the Science and Practice of Music* (London, 1776), III, 3–8, prints Cornish's setting. Hawkins' remark (p. 2) that the poem is supposed to be a satire "on those drunken Flemings who came into England with the princess Anne of Cleve, upon her marriage with king Henry VIII" can hardly be true, since Anne's marriage took place in 1540, long after Skelton's demise.

22. Dyce, I, 15–17. The poem is usually dated by means of the allusion to Perkin Warbeck. "Lord, how Perkyn is proud of hys pohen!" obviously refers to Perkin's wife, the Lady Katherine Gordon. Perkin was married in November, 1495, according to the *DNB*. For a thorough discussion of this poem in all its musical implications and aspects, see Nan C. Carpenter, "Skelton and Music: *Roty Bully Joys*," *Review of English Studies*, VI (1955), 279–84.

23. The Latin counterpart of this poem, "Contra alium cantitantem et organisantem asinum, qui impugnabat Skeltonida Pierium, Sarcas-

mos," consists of only ten lines on the erstwhile stableman, again ridiculing him in musical terms.

Apropos Skelton's upstart musician, cf. Henry William Herbert, *Memoirs of Henry the Eighth of England: with the Fortunes, Fates, and Characters of His Six Wives* (New York and Auburn, 1855), pp. 417–18 (in the midst of the account of Katherine Howard), for the story of Henry Manox, musician in the household of the Duchess of Norfolk, later a musician in the King's household, and apparently involved in Katherine's eventual downfall. In this account, Herbert gives a bitter diatribe against musicians, whom he views as "thorough profligates and villains," mixed up in "all the most disgraceful intrigues of the day."

The story of Anne Boleyn and Smeaton the musician is too well known for repetition here.

24. The play *Hyckescorner* affords a clue to the erotic meaning of this also: see fol. Av when Imagination speaks: "I mette with a wenche and she was fayre / . . . Than into loves daunce we were brought / That we played the pyrdewy." Dyce, II, 94, notes the use of the word *perdowy* in *Colkolbie Sow*.

25. This dance-song is found in a famous collection of fifteenth-century *basses danses*, MS 9085 in the Brussels Library. See the introduction and transcription by Ernest Closson, *Le Manuscrit dit des Basses Danses de la Bibliothèque de Bourgogne* (Bruxelles, 1912). For a modern transcription see Friedrich Blume, *Studien zur Vorgeschichte der Orchestersuite im 15. und 16. Jahrhundert* (Leipzig, 1925), Anhang B, p. 19.

André Pirro, "L'Enseignement de la musique aux universités françaises," *Mitteilungen der Internationalen Gesellschaft für Musikgeschichte*, II (1930), 45, quoting from the *Annales d'Avignon et du Comtat venaissin*, tells that a student in the university at Avignon in 1449 engaged a certain Jew, Mosse de Lisbonne, to teach him to play "sur la *citara sive arpa* diverses chansons: . . . *Rostit bollit.*"

26. See *The Bannatyne Manuscript*, ed. W. Tod Ritchie (Edinburgh and London, 1928–30), IV, 291.

27. Dyce, I, 249.

28. For the story of Perkin Warbeck, see the article about him by the great Tudor historian, A. F. Pollard, in the *DNB*. See also the account in Polydore Vergil's *Anglica Historia*, ed. and trans. Denys Hay (London, 1950), pp. 56–118. Martin Swart was a German nobleman in charge of soldiers sent over by the Duchess of Burgundy (patroness of Perkin) to help fight for Perkin the Pretender. He was killed at the battle of Stoke.

I can find no substantiation for the statement by E. M. Forster,

148   JOHN SKELTON

Three Cheers for Democracy (London, 1951), p. 160, that the "comely
coistroun" has been conjectured to be Lambert Simnel, who was taken
in as a kitchen-boy in the King's household after his part in the Yorkist
uprisings. Indeed, I agree with Robert Kinsman, in "Skelton's 'Uppon
a Deedmans Hed': New Light on the Origin of the Skeltonic," *Studies
in Philology*, L (1953), 104–5, that, had Skelton been satirizing a
scullery boy, he would have used other and stronger invective than
the musical terminology of the poem.

The more one studies the poem, however, the more one becomes
enchanted with the idea that the Flemish upstart might well have been
Perkin Warbeck himself: "Lord, how Perkyn is proud of hys pohen!"
The musical satire reads figuratively as well as literally. If one takes it
in the former sense, one sees strong points of similarity with the story
of Perkin. Strongest of all is the Flemish background: Perkin was born
in Tournay in 1474 and at one time in his life was associated with the
Duke of Brabant; he had many adherents in Flanders, some of whom
were executed for treason by Henry because of their association with
him; and he was under the tutelage and patronage of the old Duchess
of Burgundy (Margaret of York). One notes also the use of the pun
on *fayne*, a word often associated with Perkin's claims. Interesting, too,
is the line referring to tools for working with silk—"Wele sped in spyn-
dels and turnyng of tauellys": when Perkin landed in Cork in 1491,
much was made of the fact that he was "arrayed in fine silk clothing
which belonged to his master" (*DNB*). Many other lines in the poem
might apply to his rash actions—for example, "A malaperte medler
that pryeth for his pray, / In a dysh dare he rush at the rypest."

But nowhere can I find that Perkin actually had musical interests,
although his careful upbringing and courtly training are invariably
emphasized in accounts of his life; and these would of course have
included a thorough grounding in music. In Gainsford's *True and
Wonderful History of Perkin Warbeck*, 1618, Perkin is described as
being subtle in wit, pregnant in education, skillful in languages—also
as being effeminate: see Mildred Clara Struble, *A Critical Edition of
Ford's Perkin Warbeck* (Seattle, 1926), pp. 177 and 181, where Gainsford's account is reprinted in full as an Appendix.

29. See Dyce, II, 93.

30. *Ibid.*, I, 266. For examples of the use of this refrain in other
songs, see Joseph Ritson, *Ancient Songs and Ballads* (London, 1829),
II, 7–9. In the Chester Nativity play, the shepherds ride off singing
"Hey troly loly lo."

31. Dyce, II, 245–46.

32. See "The Libel [*libellus*] of English Policy," in Thomas Wright,
ed. *Political Poems and Songs Relating to English History* (London,
1859–61), II, 169–70: *"Of the commoditees of Pruse, and Hyghe*

Duche menne, and Esterlynges. The v. chapitle." The lines similar to Skelton's occur near the beginning of the little "chapitle" following the marginal comment, "Nota de proprietatibus et conditionibus populorum Flandrensium."

It is interesting to note that in the morality play *Nature*, by Henry Medwall (*fl.* 1486), Pride determines to turn Man into a "rutter" by clothing him elegantly:

> Sir! Our master shall have a gown
> That all the gallants, in this town,
> Shall on the fashion wonder.
>
> . . . .
> And when he is in such array—
> "There goeth a rutter," men will say;
> "A rutter, huffa gallant!"

See John S. Farmer, ed. *Recently Recovered "Lost" Tudor Plays* (London, 1907), p. 77. See also p. 287 for references to drunken Flemings in the interlude *Wealth and Health.*

33. Skelton's poem, set by Cornish, appears in *The Fayrfax Book* (B. M. MS 5465) and was printed by Hawkins in his *History of Music,* III, 9–16 (along with Cornish's setting of "Mannerly Margery," III, 3–8). "Jolly Rutterkin" was sung with great gusto and success by a men's group from Hindemith's large *collegium musicum* (of which I was happily a member) at Yale University shortly after World War II.

34. Dyce, I, 30–50. For date of the poem, see Helen Stearnes Sale, "The Date of Skelton's *Bowge of Court*," *Modern Language Notes,* LII (1937), 572–74. The colophon of one of the two existing copies (CUL) states that the book was printed by Wynken de Worde in Westminster. In 1500, Wynken moved from Westminster to Fleet Street and never returned. The book is also to be dated 1499 on the basis of the type used. Thus, Skelton could not have been influenced by Barclay's *Ship of Fools*, first published in 1508. Locher's Latin translation of Brandt's *Narrenschiff* appeared in 1497. Mrs. Sale thinks that Skelton was especially influenced by the chapters here on flattery and the vice of courtiers.

For an actual description of "bouge of court," see *A Collection of Ordinances and Regulations for the Government of the Royal Household, Made in Divers Reigns* (London, 1790), pp. 162–73: "Bouche of Court. A Declaration of Bouche of Courte, of Everie Particular Thing to be served to everie person being of the ordinary of the King's Household Honourable House, everie one of them according to their degrees" (1526). Here are carefully noted amounts of bread, ale, wine, torches, candles, faggots, wood, coal, etc., for each official, with the sum total of money to be spent during the year. Included here are members of the Chapel Royal (p. 160).

35. Dyce, II, 105–6, mentions the echo in a "noble sonnet" of Wordsworth. One finds the line in the sonnet beginning, "With ships the sea was sprinkled."

36. Joseph Ritson, *Ancient Songs and Ballads* (London, 1829), I, lxxi, quotes from Fabian's *Chronicle* (xxxii year of the reign of Henry VI):

> John Norman . . . [mayor of London] upon the . . . accustomed day when the newe mayre used yearly to ryde with great pompe unto Westminster to take his charge, this mayre first of all mayres brake that auncient and olde continued custome, & was rowed thyther by water, for the which the watermen made of hym a roundell or songe to hys great prayse, the which began, *Rowe the bote, Norman, rowe to thy lemman,* and so forthe, with a long processe.

In *Cocke Lorelles Bote* (fac. ed. Wynken de Worde, London, Roxburghe Club, 1817), fol. C. i. *verso,* we read, as the boat takes off, "For Joye theyr trumpettes dyde they blowe / And some songe heue and howe rumbelowe." This same refrain is quoted in *The Squyr of Lowe Degre:* see Joseph Ritson, ed. *Ancient English Metrical Romances* (London, 1802), III, 179: "Your maryners shall synge arowe / Hey how and rumby lowe." "Princess of Youth" is discussed in Chapter 3 below.

37. For the plainsong *O lux beata Trinitas* and a three-part polyphonic setting of the hymn tune, see Frank Lloyd Harrison, *Music in Medieval Britain* (London, 1958), pp. 150–51. Hawkins, *History of Music,* II, 354–58, gives several examples of canons upon the plainsong *O lux beata Trinitas,* which, he says (354), "seems to have been a very popular melody before the time of king Henry VIII."

38. Dyce, I, 417. Note the marginal comment beside this stanza: "Opera quæ ego facio ipsa perhibent testimonium de me: In Evang. &c."

For facts about authenticity, early publication, etc., see the discussion by Ian A. Gordon, *John Skelton, Poet Laureate* (Melbourne and London, 1943), pp. 114–16. These poems have been little discussed by Skelton's biographers; generally, their titles do not even appear in the index.

39. Dyce, I, 141–43. (See *ibid.,* II, 197, for gloss of *arrayed.*) Hawkins, *History of Music,* II, 89–90, prints the text of the poem as an "authentic specimen" of the type of song that was much sung by "the

common people," bringing them "comfort and solace" before the Psalms were translated into "the vulgar tongue."

40. For a discussion of this type of poetry and the spiritual exercises thought to have been responsible for it, see Louis L. Martz, *The Poetry of Meditation* (New Haven, 1954). Skelton, of course, is not included here.

41. For a part of Cornish's setting, see Harrison, *Music in Medieval Britain*, pp. 422–23. The date of the Fayrfax MS is c. 1500, and so Cornish obviously set the piece while he and Skelton were both at court.

42. Dyce, I, 144–46.

43. See Dom Anselm Hughes, *Early Medieval Music up to 1300* (2nd rev. impr., London, New York, Toronto, 1955), p. 80.

44. Dyce, I, 137–38. Cf. Ecclesiastes III, 2–8. Verse 17 repeats the words of the first verse: "for there is a time there for every purpose and for every work."

45. Dyce, I, 139–40.

46. *Ibid.*, I, 18–20.

47. See *Le Miroir aux Dames*, ed. Arthur Piaget (Neuchatel, 1908), p. 10. Skelton's "Myrres vous y" does not appear in this poem (although critics sometimes refer to the *Miroir* as the source of the phrase) which is not at all in the dance-of-death tradition. The phrase does occur as opening words in two poems on the mirror of death quoted by Piaget, p. 10: *Le Miroir des dames . . .* and *La Danse macabre des femmes* (or *Miroir des femmes*).

48. See Kinsman, "Uppon a Deedmans Hed," *Studies in Philology*, L, 101–9.

49. Dyce, I, 408–9.

50. *Ibid.*, I, 410–11. For the text of the treatise see Salter, "Skelton's *Speculum Principis*," *Speculum*, IX, 33–37. The treatise has never been translated. For a discussion of its contents, see Nelson, pp. 90–101, where the medieval *Reimprosa* tradition is thoroughly gone into. See also Edwards, pp. 73–75, where bits of the treatise are translated.

51. Thomas Wilson in *The Arte of Rhetorique* (London, 1553), fol. 108, has a section on "Lyke endyng, and lyke fallyng." In it he speaks of ancient times, when the people "were so nyce & so waiwarde to please, that excepte the Preacher from tyme to tyme coulde ryme out his Sermon, they woulde not long abide the hearyng." And he continues, "I know some in this our time do ouermuch vse them in their writynges. And ouermuche (as al men know) was neuer good yet."

52. See, for example, Gordon, *Skelton*, p. 93.

53. Dyce, I, 168–73. For identification of the two knaves and facts of their lives in Diss, see Nelson, pp. 103–4, and Edwards, pp. 92–

94. There were two men in Diss called John Clark, one a priest and the other not.

54. Edwards (93–94) has essayed to turn a few of these Latin verses into English Skeltonics. The Latin is so easy that anyone may read it with the help of a dictionary. The feast of John implies a pun, of course, in these lines, "Let us sing songs with reed pipes on the feast of John." Note the nautical refrain "Hey, ho, rumblelow!" (see note 36 above) mixed in with bits of the plainsong here.

55. Dyce, I, 174.

56. *Ibid.*, I, 51–94. For full information about Jane's family and their connection with Skelton, see Edwards, pp. 102–14.

57. Alexander Barclay, *The Ship of Fooles* (London, 1570), fol. 259.

58. Bird Masses developed along with Venus Masses as part of the courtly love tradition. See Gordon, *Skelton*, pp. 122–23. P. Lehman, *Die Parodie im Mittelalter* (Munich, 1922) is a standard source here. See also Dyce, II, 121, for early examples of the Bird Mass.

Among poems sometimes attributed to Skelton (although no longer considered authentic) is a unique poem in which many birds take part in a concert "Praisyng our Lorde, / Without discorde, / With goodly armony"—*A Proper New Boke of The Armony of Byrdes* (London, 1843). Here the various birds sing parts of the service.

59. See Salter and Edwards, *Diodorus Siculus*, II, xxxix–xl, for a comparison with the *Poetria Nova.*

60. Gordon, *Skelton*, pp. 119–34, has a good discussion of Skelton and the Goliardic tradition. "*Philip Sparow* is best regarded as two related poems," says Gordon (p. 132), "the first of which, containing the lament, the Requiem Mass, the Office for the Dead and the Absolution over the Tomb, is goliardic both in spirit and execution." A major collection of Goliardic verse is the *Carmina Burana*, a thirteenth-century MS from the monastery at Benediktbeuern. See Gustave Reese, *Music in the Middle Ages* (New York, 1940), pp. 200–1, for other sources.

61. Dyce, I, 411–12.

62. Gordon, *Skelton*, pp. 121–34, has a most thorough and complete discussion of the poem in its relation to the Roman service books. Skelton's accurate use of breviary and missal is closely followed, lines in the poem from the services are identified, and Skelton's originality with the Bird Mass is described. Gordon (p. 132) sums up Skelton's usage by noting these divisions and their correlation with the services for the dead: *Officium Defunctorum* (Breviary), 1–386; *Missa pro Defunctis* (Missal), 387–512; *Absolutio super Tumulum* (Missal), 513–70; *Officium Defunctorum* (Breviary), 571–602; *Ordo Commendationis Animae* (Breviary), 845–1260.

For a short, contemporary parody of the Requiem Mass, see William Dunbar's "Dirige to the King at Stirling," Laing, *Poems of Dunbar*, I, 86–90. Laing calls this "a profane parody of the Services of the Church" and quotes Lord Hailes's words that the piece "is a lewd and profane parody of the litanies of the Church of Rome:" see II, 279–81.

An earlier poem of this type is the Requiem "On the Death of the Duke of Suffolk" (May 3, 1450), in Thomas Wright, *Political Poems and Songs* (London, 1859–61), II, 232–34, and in Ritson, *Ancient Songs and Ballads*, I, 117–20.

One might mention, too, that less than a half-century after *Philip Sparrow*, the Requiem Mass was used as background for a boisterous funeral scene in *Ralph Roister Doister*, apparently giving offense to no one and pleasure to many. See Act III, scene iii, and see Nan C. Carpenter, "*Ralph Roister Doister: Miles* vs. *clericus*," *Notes and Queries*, VII (1960), 168–70.

63. For a most interesting explanation of this genre of literature and its reflection in *Philip Sparrow*, see Robert S. Kinsman, "*Phyllyp Sparowe: Titulus*," *Studies in Philology*, XLVII (1950), 473–84.

64. See Dyce, II, 120–21, for Ovid, Catullus, Chaucer, etc., and for the Coleridge reference below (*Remains*, II, 163).

65. Dyce, I, 155–67.

66. A portion of Skelton's old church at Diss still stands. Nelson once took a good look around and discovered that one could have got in when the door was locked by going up into the tower and descending into the nave through another door: see p. 105 n.

Apparently Skelton's cleric was not the only one who brought hawks and hounds to church. See, for example, Barclay's *Ship of Fooles*, in the section "Of them that make noyses, rehearsinges of tales, and do other thinges vnlawfull and dishonest in the Churche of God" (ed. 1570, fol. 85):

Into the Church then comes another sotte,
. . . .
Another on his fiste a Sparhauke or Fawcone.

. . . .
In comes another his houndes at his tayle,
With lynes and leases and other like baggage,
His dogges barke, so that withouten fayle,
The whole Church is troubled by their outrage.

. . . .
One time the hawkes belles iangleth hye,
Another time they flutter with their winges,
And nowe the houndes barking strikes the skye,
Nowe sounde their feete, and nowe the chaynes ringes,

They clap with their handes: by suche maner thinges
They make of the Church for their hawkes a mewe,
And Canell for their dogges, which they shall after rewe.

67. One John Smith was Rector of East Wretham from 1503 until 1517. Since this town is only fifteen miles from Diss, its rector may perhaps have been the offending parson. See Edwards, pp. 91–92. Edwards points out that the word *curate* was at that time the equivalent of *parson* or *rector*.

68. Bradley's solution was published in the *Academy*, August 1, 1896. See Nelson, p. 106 n.

69. A. R. Heiserman, *Skelton and Satire* (Chicago, 1961), p. 281.

70. Both Dyce (I, 148–54) and Henderson print a poem long attributed to Skelton, which may date from this time: *The Maner of the World Now a Dayes*. In short stanzas, each repeating (twice) the refrain "Sawe I never," *repetitio* is powerfully used to build up the idea of so little good and so much evil in the world. The poem is, in fact, one long catalogue in which "so few" good things and people are contrasted with "so many" bad things—as in

> So many lollers [heretics]
> So few true tollers [tellers, speakers]
> So many baudes and pollers [plunderers],
>   Sawe I never;
> Such treachery,
> Simony and usury,
> Poverty and lechery,
> Saw I never.

Dyce, II, 199–203, prints what is evidently the source of the poem, verses from MS Sloane 747, of which the later poem is simply a *rifacimento*. Skelton's *Maner of the World*, if it is his, is nearly twice as long as the original, but otherwise quite similar.

71. Dyce, I, 191. For a discussion of *Salve, festa dies* as a processional hymn and for excerpts from both plainsong and polyphonic settings of it, see Harrison, *Music in Medieval Britain*, pp. 403–6. See also Manfred Bukofzer. *Studies in Medieval Music* (New York, 1950), pp. 113 ff., and see illustrations of three-part polyphonic settings, p. 142. For the form of the processional hymn, see Gustave Reese, *Music in the Renaissance* (New York, 1954), p. 336.

72. Dyce, I, 190. Holinshed, *Chronicles*, III, 588, describes the festivities on this occasion.

73. See Ashton, *A Ballade of the Scottysshe Kynge*, pp. 91–96, for

a facsimile reproduction of the only extant copy of the poem. Ashton's excellent introduction discusses all circumstances of the political events, the poem, etc. Dyce does not include the *Ballade* in his edition.

On the basis of certain points connected with these poems on the victory over the Scots, Edwards argues that Skelton was at home, performing his duties as *"orator reginae:"* see pp. 139–43.

74. For a description of this event, see Holinshed, *Chronicles*, III, 581 ff. Nelson, pp. 129–33, gives a summary, making the interesting point—quite rightly, it seems to me—that since several of the contemporary accounts (Hall's *Chronicle,* MS Harleian 2252) are so very similar to Skelton's, his may easily have been the first and official account, which was later copied by the historians.

75. Dyce, I, 182–89.

76. *Ibid.,* I, 192–94. Dyce (II, 224) identifies the subject of this tirade as the Scottish knight, George Dundas, professor at Aberdeen, who flourished about 1520; and he suggests that the three Latin hexameters (saying Englishmen have tails) with which the poem opens were written by Dundas. Cf. the superscription: "Vilitissimus Scotus Dundas Allegat Caudas Contra Angligenas." Dyce also traces in great detail the history of the old saying that Kentishmen had tails (II, 224–225).

77. *Ibid.,* I, 116–31.

78. See Laing, *Poems of Dunbar,* I, 13 and 28. *The Flyting of Dunbar and Kennedy* may be found in II, 63–86. For information about the history of this literary form, see Laing's notes, II, 417–20. It is pointed out here that a flyting need not arise from personal animosity: Dunbar and Kennedy were actually good friends. Laing also notes that the poems abound with allusions to the personal history of both men, a trait we see imitated in Skelton's *Poems Against Garnesche.* Dyce, II, 177–94, notices similar details in the two poems, but I do not find that the poems have ever been compared in depth.

For facts about Garnesche's family and career and for date of the flyting, see Helen Stearnes Sales, "John Skelton and Christopher Garnesche," *Modern Language Notes,* XLIII (1928), 518–23.

79. Laing, *Poems of Dunbar,* I, 28, cites the notice from Henry VII's Privy Purse Expenses stating that "The Rhymer of Scotland" received £6/13/4 from the King on December 31, 1501, and a similar sum on January 7, 1502. One must multiply by at least forty to reckon the equivalent today.

80. Godfrey has never been identified. Ian Gordon, *London Times Literary Supplement,* Nov. 15, 1934, p. 795, suggested that he might represent Stephen Hawes, creator of Godfrey Gobelive, a mischievous dwarf in the *Pastime of Pleasure.* Nelson, p. 145, thought Godfrey might be Godfrey Gormand, a "scurrilous fellow" found in Barclay's

Miseries of Courtiers (written c. 1513). Edwards, pp. 149–55, has an interesting account of Garnesche and agrees with Gordon that Godfrey probably represented Hawes.

81. See note 47 above.

82. Dyce, I, 408–9.

83. See Thomas Warton, *History of English Poetry* (London, 1774–81), II, 360–63, for a description of the play: *The Nigramansir, a morall Enterlude and a pithie written by Maister Skelton laureate and plaid before the king and other estatys at Woodstoke on Palme Sunday.* Warton claims to have seen a copy belonging to William Collins. Warton's summary of the play (sometimes thought to have been an elaborate hoax: cf., for example, Edwards, p. 169) is quite detailed:

> The characters are a Necromancer, or conjurer, the devil, a notary public, Simonie, and Philargyria, or Avarice. It is partly a satire on some abuses in the church; yet not without a due regard to decency, and an apparent respect for the dignity of the audience. The story, or plot, is the tryal of Simony and Avarice: the devil is the judge, and the notary public acts as an assessor or scribe. The prisoners, as we may suppose, are found guilty, and ordered into hell immediately. There is no sort of propriety in calling this play the Necromancer: for the only business and use of this character, is to open the subject in a long prologue, to evoke the devil, and summon the court. The devil kicks the necromancer, for waking him so soon in the morning: a proof, that this drama was performed in the morning, perhaps in the chapel of the palace. A variety of measures, with shreds of Latin and French, is used: but the devil speaks in the octave stanza. One of the stage-directions is, *Enter Balsebub with a Berde.* To make him both frightful and ridiculous, the devil was most commonly introduced on the stage, wearing a visard with an immense beard. Philargyria quotes Seneca and saint Austin: and Simony offers the devil a bribe. The devil rejects her offer with much indignation: and swears by the *foule Eumenides,* and the hoary beard of Charon, that she shall be well fried and roasted in the unfathomable sulphur of Cocytus, together with Mahomet, Pontius Pilate, the traitor Judas, and king Herod. The last scene is closed with a view of hell, and a dance between the devil and the necromancer. The dance ended, the devil trips up the necromancer's heels, and disappears in fire and smoke. Great must have been the edification and entertainment which king Henry the seventh and his court derived from the exhibition of so elegant and rational a drama!

Pollard, *Wolsey*, p. 101, speaks of Wolsey's terrific influence over Henry VIII: "The fascination Wolsey exerted over his mind was attributed by the discontented to witchcraft," and he adds in a note: "Skelton wrote a lost drama, entitled *The Nigramansir* (Dyce, ii. 355) which probably dealt with Wolsey." If Warton, however, was correct in reporting that the lost play was printed in 1504, it could hardly have been aimed at Wolsey, who did not become a royal chaplain until 1507 and who was appointed to his first office (royal almoner) under Henry VIII in November, 1509 (see *ibid.*, p. 13).

84. Dyce, I, 225–310. Any discussion of the play must take its start from the painstaking analysis by Robert Lee Ramsay, *Magnyfycence* (EETS, London, 1906). Lloyd, *Skelton*, pp. 76–98, devotes a whole chapter to the play, as does Gordon, *Skelton*, pp. 135–46. For the French, there is a lengthy discussion in Pollet, *Skelton*, pp. 104–27. The chapter on *Magnyfycence* in Heiserman, *Skelton and Satire*, pp. 66–125, although drawing heavily upon Ramsay, investigates in some detail certain "key ideas" found in the play (ideas "of the flattering counsellor, of king and anti-king, of foolish and measured largess") and also what Heiserman calls the "now-a-days" *topos* (103). Heiserman disallows (123) Aristotelian influence, long held to be quite strong in *Magnificence*.

85. On this aspect of the satire, see Ramsay, *Magnyfycence*, pp. cvi ff. For sources of the play, see *ibid.*, pp. lxxi–lxxxix. For date, see *ibid.*, pp. xxi–xxv. The reader curious as to why Skelton implies that Francis I was not a lavish spender will welcome Ramsay's explanation that in *Magnificence*, "we are certainly looking at the first five years of Francis's reign, and, moreover, through hostile English eyes." Eyes were hostile because Louis's "largesse" to his betrothed, Henry's sister, became the subject of a long controversy when the French King died and Henry demanded the restoration of Mary's dowry. "Naturally," says Ramsay, "the reputation of Francis for liberality was at a low ebb in England after these transactions"—all of which Skelton cleverly capitalized upon.

86. See *ibid.*, pp. xxvi–xxviii, and see Ramsay's edition of the play. Henderson uses Ramsay's stage and scene divisions in his edition of the poems, pp. 165–244.

87. For a discussion of the two types of fools, see Ramsay, *Magnyfycence*, pp. xcvii–cii. The difference between natural and artificial fool is plainly illustrated in Lear's Fool and Touchstone or Feste.

88. I am sure that if Courtly Abusion is meant to portray any particular person at court, it is the same person called earlier the Comely Coistrown. Many of the same overtones characterize these two. For the many Flemish names among the royal musicians during the reigns of

Henry VII and Henry VIII, see Henry Cart de LaFontaine, *The King's Musick* (London, 1909), pp. 1–8.

89. See Ramsay, *Magnyfycence*, pp. li–lxxi, for a detailed study of versification. Ramsay, pp. cxxxiv–cxlvii, compares Skelton's versification to that of the other morality plays (*Castle of Perseverance, Wisdom, Mankind, Nature, Four Elements, Everyman, Hickscorner,* and others) and finds Skelton far ahead of the rest in developing new forms and in using old ones in an original way.

90. T. W. Craik, *The Tudor Interlude* (Leicester, 1958), p. 87, makes the point that the spiritual theme of the play is emphasized through changes in clothing (Magnificence beaten down and in rags is given new clothing when restored to his crown and wealth), whereas in later political plays the costume-change is treated "purely in terms of material rehabilitation."

91. Even on the word *sight* there is a musical pun. Singing at sight upon a given tenor was a favorite with the British—that is, improvising in thirds and sixths (in treble and mean) so as to harmonize over a given melody (tenor) line. See Nan C. Carpenter, "Music in the *Secunda Pastorum*," *Speculum*, XXVI (1951), 696–700, for a famous application of this in literature.

92. Dyce, I, 132–36. Dyce prints the continual Latin gloss, based on the Psalms and ancient writers, along with the poem. The line "I made, he said, a windmil of an olde mat" is echoed in *Magnificence* in Fancy's speech, "Nowe I wyll this, and nowe I wyll that; / Make a wyndmyll of a mat."

93. Edwards, pp. 163–67. See also Cavendish's description, note 106 below.

94. Pollet, *Skelton*, pp. 107–9. For an understanding of these events, Pollard, *Wolsey*, is indispensable: see pp. 72–78 for an account of Wolsey's Star Chamber and other activities against the aristocracy. See p. 76 for the business of retainers. Dr. Rowse, a great admirer of Wolsey, has pointed out to me (at the Caltech Athenaeum dinner table) that the King could not afford to have any one lord become too strong—hence these restrictive measures.

95. Dyce, II, 1–25. *Speke, Parrot* has been most thoroughly glossed and investigated than any other single work by Skelton; and yet there is still no completely satisfactory study of the poem. John Berdan was the first to study the poem at any length in "'Speke, Parrot': An Interpretation of Skelton's Satire," *Modern Language Notes*, XXX (1915), 140–44. Nelson (158–84) and Edwards (182–208) have excellent discussions of the poem, including an explanation of the figures 33 and 34 at the end of the first and second envoys, which help to establish the date of the poem and of Skelton's private calendar. Heiserman, *Skelton and Satire*, has a detailed *explication de texte* (126–65) fol-

lowed by a comparison of *Speke, Parrot* with conventional satires (165–89). Pollet, *Skelton* (144–54), includes a discussion of the poem.

96. For an explanation of Parrot as a bird of Paradise, see Edwards, pp. 182–84.

97. For a description of the contents of commonplace books, see Henry A. Person, ed. *Cambridge Middle English Lyrics* (Seattle, 1962) p. iv.

98. Edwards, pp. 191–93, believes Besse stands for mankind and that the speaker here (Parrot) is the "vehicle of religious truth"; that the ballad is a pious allegory representing "Christ's lament over the fickleness of humanity." The old English ballad, "Come over the burn, Besse," may be found in William Chappell, *Popular Music of Olden Times* (London, 1855–59), I, 122.

For "The Most Pleasant Song of Lady Bessy," by Humphrey Brereton, see the edition by James Orchard Halliwell (Percy Society, London, 1847). The poem is analyzed at great length by Agnes Strickland, *Lives of the Queens of England* (London, 1842–48), IV, 9 ff.

It is interesting to note that the Queen herself had a "royal popinjay," for which she paid thirteen shillings and fourpence, a considerable sum when multiplied by forty or more (for today's equivalent). See Nicolas, *Privy Purse Expenses of Elizabeth of York*, p. 30 (July, 1502): "Item the same day to a servaunt of William ap Howell for bringing of a popyngay to the Quene to Windesore xiij s. iiij d."

99. See Person, *Cambridge Lyrics*, pp. 65–66, for various types of ABC poems.

100. See Nelson, pp. 165–71, for an analysis of these envoys and the historical events behind them.

101. This section of the poem is very similar to "A General Satyre," by William Dunbar, with the refrain, "Within this land was nevir hard nor sene." See Laing, *Poems of Dunbar*, II, 24–27.

102. See Edwards, pp. 197–208 for identification of Skelton's patroness and the circumstances of this patronage.

103. Wolsey himself admitted this to the French chancellor in 1521: see Pollard, *Wolsey*, p. 316.

104. See John Holloway, *The Charted Mirror* (London, 1960), pp. 21–22.

105. Dyce, I, 311–60. For Francis Thynne's story that *Colyn Cloute* was largely written at the home of William Thynne, chief clerk of the kitchen for Henry VIII, see Edwards, pp. 208–10. John Berdan, *Early Tudor Poetry* (New York, 1920) and all of Skelton's biographers discuss the poem. Robert Kinsman has an interesting interpretation in *Essays Dedicated to Lily B. Campbell* (Berkeley, 1950): "Skelton's 'Colyn Cloute': The Mask of 'Vox Populi.'" See also the very detailed

study of the poem by Robert Kinsman, "The Voices of Dissonance: Pattern in Skelton's *Colyn Cloute*," *The Huntington Library Quarterly*, XXVI (1963), 291–313. Heiserman, *Skelton and Satire*, pp. 190–243, examines the poem in great detail (disagreeing with many points made by Nelson and Edwards) and evaluates it in the light of its literary antecedents.

106. Cavendish in his *Life of Wolsey* (Boston and New York, 1905), plays up this side of the Cardinal. His most often quoted passage is this one (45):

> Then marched he forward out of his own house at Westminster, passing through all London, over London Bridge, having before him of gentlemen a great number, three in a rank, in black velvet livery coats, and the most part of them with great chains of gold about their necks, and all his yeomen, with noblemen's and gentlemen's servants following him in French tawny livery coats; having embroidered upon the backs and breasts of the said coats these letters: T. and C., under the cardinal's hat. . . . He rode like a cardinal, very sumptuously, on a mule trapped with crimson velvet upon velvet, and his stirrups of copper and gilt; and his spare mule following him with like apparel. And before him he had his two great crosses of silver, two great pillars of silver, the great seal of England, his cardinal's hat. . . . Thus passed he through London. . . .

107. For explanation of this, see Dyce, I, 329.

108. See Edwards, p. 215, for an explanation of which tapestries are meant.

109. We owe these discoveries to Nelson: see p. 190.

110. See *Letters and Papers*, III, nos. 634, 647, 676.

111. Dyce, I, 95–115. *Elinor Rumming* is unique among Skelton's major works, in fact, in that its date is still uncertain. It was long thought to have been written during the Diss period because it resembles *Philip Sparrow* in many respects and because it lacks the *orator regius* endorsement: see Gordon, p. 74.

Pollet, (*Skelton*, p. 130) argues rather convincingly for the year 1517 on the basis of topical allusions in the passage,

> Than thyder came dronken Ales;
> And she was full of tales,
> Of tydynges in Wales,
> And of sainct James in Gales,
> And of the Portyngales;
> . . . .

> There hath ben great war
> Betwene Temple Bar
> And the Crosse in Chepe,
> And there came an hepe
> Of mylstones in a route. . . .

In 1517 there was a "war" on between native and foreign merchants, tradesmen, and artificers, which resulted in riots in the City. A good account of all this and the way the riots were cruelly put down may be found in J. S. Brewer, *The Reign of Henry VIII* (London, 1884), I, 243–49. Moreover, the court was moved to Richmond, Surrey, in May of this year because of the sweating sickness, and the Portuguese ambassador had an audience with the King at Richmond on May 10. See *Letters and Papers of Henry VIII*, II, ii (1517), 3204 and 3218.

Edwards (122–24) dates the poem 1522 because of its stylistic resemblance to *Colin Clout* and because of the relationship he thinks it bears to the *Garland of Laurel*. In support of Edwards' argument, I might add that Charles V was in England during May and June, 1522, and that the idea uppermost in his mind was the union of Spain and Portugal (see Brewer, *Henry VIII*, I, 453–54). However, Skelton might easily have added Wales and Portingales for the sake of the rhyme. He might also have had "drunken Alice" speak of events of years past as if they happened yesterday.

It also appears that the poem might even date back to about the time of Henry's ascension and Skelton's various gifts to the new King in the hope of obtaining royal favor. In the Latin distichon following the poem, the poet begs to be remembered in the phrase used on these presentation poems: *Bien men souuient (Bien m'en souvient)*. And at the end of the Latin verses he writes simply, "Quod Skelton, Laureat." Since the *orator regius* used the title given him in 1512–13 by the King on most of the poems written after that time, one wonders why it is missing here if the poem was written after 1512.

112. See Edwards, p. 115. Edwards notes that one branch of the Skelton family lived at Reigate, in Surrey. He also notes that in 1525 "Alionora Romyng, common tippler of ale," was certified by the Leatherhead ale-taster for short-changing her customers and fined for it. This, too, perhaps strengthens Edwards' arguments for a late dating of the poem.

113. The Latin is much more forceful than my translation: *"Ebria, squalida, sordida fœmina, prodiga verbis, / Huc currat, properet, veniat! Sua gesta libellus / Iste volutabit: Pæan sua plectra sonando / Materiam risus cantabit carmine rauco."*

114. Gordon is the only one of Skelton's biographers who has noticed this edition: see p. 201.

115. See Gordon, p. 77, and Nelson, p. 50. For an excellent appreciation of the poem, see Lloyd, *Skelton,* pp. 60–65.

116. *The Charted Mirror,* p. 9. Holloway's account of *Elinor Rumming,* although brief, is highly perceptive: see pp. 7–11.

117. Laing, *Poems of Dunbar,* I, 102–4.

118. Pollet, *Skelton,* p. 131, is the first to point out similarities between the two poems. For the older poem, see Thomas Wright, *Songs and Carols* (Percy Society, London, 1847), pp. 91–95. Pollet, appendix II, pp. 251–54, prints the two poems side by side.

119. The stories involving Skelton are printed by Dyce, I, lxxxi–lxxxv. Skelton is also associated with Will Sommers, Henry VIII's famous fool, in Samuel Rowley's play, *When You See Me, You Know Me* (1605): see fol. A4 (facsimile edition, Oxford, 1952). See pp. 125–126 below.

120. Dyce, I, 411.

121. Nelson, p. 120.

122. Dyce, II, 26–67.

123. Edwards, p. 219.

124. See Brewer, *Henry VIII,* I, 451–97 and Pollard, *Wolsey,* 132 ff.

125. Pollard, *Wolsey,* p. 325n.

126. *Ibid.,* p. 221, and see Brewer, *Henry VIII,* II, 206, where the letter is quoted in English: "The Archbishop of Canterbury never comes to Court, unless compelled, on account of the Legate."

127. See Pollard, *Wolsey,* pp. 79 and 77.

128. See Gordon, *Skelton,* pp. 161–62, for identification of some eight references in the poem, from October, 1522 until March, 1523. Edwards' rebuttal of this dating is most unconvincing (282–83), but Edwards is determined to prove that the poem was completed before January, 1523.

129. See Brewer, *Henry VIII,* I, 465, 494, etc.; Pollard, *Wolsey,* pp. 121 ff; and see the many documents relating to the war in *Letters and Papers,* IV.

130. For an account of this Parliament, see Brewer, *Henry VIII,* I, 469–97 and Pollard, *Wolsey,* pp. 132 ff.

131. See Pollard, *Wolsey,* pp. 192–94.

132. *Ibid.,* p. 145.

133. Robert Kinsman. "The 'Buck' and the 'Fox' in Skelton's *Why Come Ye Nat to Courte?*" *Philological Quarterly,* XXIX (1950), 61–64, agrees with the wider dating of the poem, October, 1522–March, 1523. Heiserman, who in *Skelton and Satire* devotes a chapter to the poem as invective in the *sirventes* tradition, contradicts himself: he dates it October, 1522 on p. 271 and 1522–23 on p. 245.

134. See Dyce, I, lxxx, for the excerpt from John Chamber, *A Treatise Against Judicial Astrologie,* 1601: "Not much vnlike to merrie

Skelton, who thrust his wife out at the doore, and receiued her in againe at the window. The storie is well known how the bishop had charged him to thrust his wife out of the doore: but that which was but a merriment in Skelton . . ." (p. 99).

135. For the 44 articles, see Herbert, *Henry VIII*, pp. 294–302. No. VI. has to do with Wolsey's "foul disease," but I cannot find reference anywhere to the fact that he had the use of only one eye:

VI. And also, whereas your Grace is our Sovereign Lord and Head, in whom standeth all the Surety and Wealth of this Realm, the same Lord Cardinal knowing himself to have the foul and contagious Disease of the Great Pox, broken out upon him in divers places of his Body, came daily to your Grace, rowning in your ear, and blowing upon your most Noble Grace with his perillous and infective Breath, to the marvellous danger of your Highness, if God of his infinite Goodness had not better provided for your Highness. And when he was once healed of them, he made your Grace to believe that his Disease was an Impostume in his head, and of none other thing.

The articles are reprinted in *Letters and Papers*, IV (iii), 2712–14, no. 6075. The articles are signed by Thomas More, the Dukes of Norfolk and Suffolk, the Earls of Dorset, Oxford, Northumberland, etc. Pollard, *Wolsey*, pp. 258–60, summarizes the articles. He also notes (p. 259) that some of these lords had earlier compiled lists of charges against Wolsey from which they selected the articles brought against him in 1529.

136. Dyce, I, 361–427. Both Nelson (190–92) and Edwards (226–228) had the astrological bit worked out and both date the astrological reference at the beginning of the poem January, 1523.

137. This suggestion has been made by Lloyd, p. 123; Henderson, *Poems*, p. 372; Edwards, p. 239; and Pollet, p. 173. My research into the facts of the poet's life leads me to believe that he was actually living in peace and safety with the Howards while writing his long works of 1521–23.

138. Although it is sometimes suggested that Skelton had more than a passing glance at Bocaccio's *De mulieribus claris* in listing women from antiquity here, only six of Skelton's fifteen are to be found in Bocaccio's work. See *Libri Johanni boccacij de Certaldo de mulieribus claris* (Ulm, 1473 [for 1475]).

139. For a handy listing of Skelton's lost works (based on the *Garland*), see Lloyd, *Skelton*, pp. 142–43.

140. See Dyce, I, 424–25.

141. See *ibid.*, I, xl and xlix.

164   JOHN SKELTON

142. *Ibid.*, II, 68–84. For the political background of the poem, see
ibid., II, 375–77. See also the numerous documents in *Letters and
Papers*, III, ii, 1393 ff., from late September, 1523, onwards, telling of
Albany's plans for invading England and of Surrey's plans for defense
of his country. See also Brewer, *Henry VIII*, I, 553–64.

143. Dyce, I, 206–23. For background of the poem, see Edwards,
pp. 244–46. J. B. Mullinger first identified the young heretical scholars: see his *University of Cambridge* (Cambridge, 1873), I, 607–8.

144. Dyce (II, 83–84) publishes this Envoy after the poem on the
Duke of Albany, although he notes that the Envoy does not belong
with the poem. See Chapter 1 above.

145. This similarity was first pointed out by Nelson: see pp. 215–
216.

Chapter Three

1. C. S. Lewis, *English Literature in the Sixteenth Century* (Oxford, 1954), p. 143.

2. Introduction to Skelton's *Complete Poems*, pp. xi–xii.

3. To Bulman, Whittington, and Skelton. See Salter and Edwards,
Diodorus Siculus, II, xxxiv.

4. See F. M. Salter, *John Skelton's Contribution to the English Lan-
guage* (Ottawa, 1945), Transactions of the Royal Society of Canada,
Third Series, XXXIX, section 2. This article has been summarized in
Diodorus Siculus, II, xxxii–xxxiv.

5. For Skelton as humanist, one must not fail to read the accounts
by Nelson, pp. 40–58, and Edwards, pp. 15–28. Gordon, too, pp. 82–
101, has a good summary. The latest and best account of Skelton as a
rhetorician is that of Salter and Edwards, *Diodorus Siculus*, II, xxxiv-
liii.

6. Gordon, p. 96, reminds us that it was Wolsey who founded the
Oxford lectureship in Greek and suggests that the Cardinal's great enthusiasm for the subject was one reason for Skelton's "stand against the
too easy introduction of Greek."

7. Nelson, pp. 82–101, remains the best discussion of the origin of
the Skeltonic, but there are of course discussions of this subject in all
books about Skelton.

8. The poet W. H. Auden has noted this and remarked on it in his
chapter on Skelton in *The Great Tudors*, ed. Katherine Garvin (London, 1935), pp. 62–63: "The skeltonic is such a simple metre that it
is surprising that fewer poets have not used it. The natural unit of
speech rhythm seems to be one of four accents, dividing into two half
verses of two accents. If one tries to write ordinary conversation in
verse, it will fall more naturally into this scheme than into any other.
. . . Skelton is said to have spoken as he wrote, and his skeltonics

have the natural ease of speech rhythm." The "sprung rhythm" of Gerard Manley Hopkins turns out to be nothing new—simply Skelton's principle of speech rhythm rediscovered.

9. For sequences, see Reese, *Music in the Middle Ages*, pp. 187 ff. The eleventh-century sequence *Lætabundus,* says Reese (189), "became the model for over a hundred imitations."

10. There are two polyphonic settings of songs with this refrain in BM Add. MS 31922 ("Henry VIII's MS"): see Stevens, *Music and Poetry in the Early Tudor Court,* p. 438. All the pieces in this collection are printed in *Music at the Court of Henry VIII,* ed. John Stevens, *Musica Britannica,* XVIII (London, 1962). This collection also includes a three-part setting of "Trolly lolly" by Skelton's associate William Cornish (no. 39).

Many of these song-tags have been mentioned in the course of this work, and their use in the poems of other writers noted. Unfortunately, few of them can be identified musically and by no means all of them can be identified textually. For instance, I have been unable to find anywhere words or music to a song mentioned three times by Skelton (*Bouge of Court, Why Come Ye? Devout Trental*): "In faith, deacon, thou crew." And there are four references to singing *Welaway* (*Colin Clout, Speak, Parrot, Replication, Ballad of Scottish King*) which is found in several of the medieval cycle plays also. Is this the title of a song? I have been unable to find any trace of it.

11. This chanson has been described by Manfred Bukofzer, "The First English Chanson on the Continent" (revised title: "An Early English Chanson on the Continent": see *Musical Quarterly,* XXVIII [1942], 14) in *Music and Letters,* XIX (1938), 119. The piece survives in an anonymous three-part setting in the Chansonnier of the Escorial. Bukofzer notes that the words were written down by a scribe who did not understand English, and are very corrupt. They seem to be: "Princesse of youth, and flowre of godlihede, / The perfect miror of all gentilnesse."

12. Dyce, I, 249. An anonymous 2-part instrumental version of *Votre trey dowce* is found in the so-called Ritson MS in the British Museum (BM Add. MS 5665): see Stevens, *Music and Poetry,* p. 348.

13. For references to the harp and harping (Latin *lyra*), see *Philip Sparrow,* ll. 863–66; *Colin Clout,* ll. 492–93; *Garland of Laurel,* ll. 272–74 and 687–88; *Replication,* ll. 338–46, and also the Latin glosses found in Dyce, I, 219 and 220.

14. This system, used from the time of Guido d'Arezzo, was based upon seven interlocking hexachords, each containing six tones called by Guido's *voces* (vocables) *ut, re, mi, fa, sol, la,* and ranging from G (*gamma ut:* in modern terms, G on the first line of the bass staff) to E (*la:* E in the fourth space of the treble staff). See diagram in Car-

penter, *Rabelais and Music*, pp. 80–81. It will be noticed that Skelton's *A-la-mi-re* occurs twice in the scale, once in the middle register (where it would cause no comment) and once in the highest register—much too high for the ordinary man's voice.

15. See the listing of words used by Skelton antedating the first usage in the OED. in Salter, *Skelton's Contribution to the English Language.*

16. See lines quoted, p. 146 above. Skelton refers to St. Jerome's Epistle to Paul and immediately quotes from this *verbatim: "Dauid, inquit,"* etc. See the beautiful volumes, edited by Erasmus, in the Huntington Library, *Omnium Operum Divi Eusebii Hieronymi* (Basileam, 1516–20), IV, fol. 3 *verso.* In the same volume (fol. 5) a "Scholia in epistola ad Paulinum" identifies the poets mentioned by Jerome (and cited by Skelton).

17. For instance, one of Rabelais' most effective musical metaphors describes the storm at sea in terms of tones of the gamut, as Panurge, deeply frightened, pictures the rise and fall of the ship on the waves: "Zalas, zalas! nous sommes au dessus de E la, hors toute la gamme. Bebe be bous bous. Zalas! à ceste heure sommes nous au dessous de Gamma ut." See *Les Oeuvres complètes de Rabelais,* ed. Jean Plattard (Paris, 1929), IV, xix.

18. See Carpenter, *Music in the Medieval and Renaissance Universities, passim.*

Actually, the one time Skelton seems to be out of his depth musically is in translating several Greek terms in Poggio's *Diodorus Siculus,* when he fails to clarify musical terms for his readers but refers, in an offhand way, to the specialists (the music faculty). Poggio, I, 303, states quite simply: "Ad hanc postmodum muse linus quam lichanon orpheus & Tamyrus quam hypaten ac parhypaten, musici dicunt addiderunt." The laureate's translation of this has long puzzled editors and critics. (In his earlier work, *Skelton's Contribution to the English Language,* p. 181, Salter confesses that he cannot determine Skelton's exact meaning. In *Diodorus,* I, 303, the key word is left unglossed.) Says Skelton, "Aftre, by contynuaunce of yeres, the Muses of theire enstynctions divyne adioyned vnto this enstrument menyall strynges; and Lynes, Orpheus, and Tamyrus, they annexed swete vnysions and coordes of melodious sownde which musicions in their facultie call hippates."

Hippates is not difficult to gloss in the light of what we know today of ancient Greek music—and it is, of course, perfectly clear in Poggio's version. *Hypate* and *parhypate* are simply the names of tones in the highest tetrachord—in our sense, the lowest, since the Greeks used a descending scale —in the so-called Greater Perfect System of musical intervals and tones. This system is described by Boethius: see Reese, *Music in the Middle Ages,* pp. 21–23.

Oldfather in the Loeb Classical Library (cited in a note, *Diodorus,* I, 303), gives a straightforward translation: "This harmony of the strings, however, was rediscovered, when the Muses added later the middle string, Linus the string struck with the forefinger, and Orpheus and Thamyres the lowest string and the one next to it." Actually, there is a mistake here: Proslambanomenos was the lowest string, Hypate next to it, and Parhypate next to that. For easy reference, see Boethius' explanatory diagram in Carpenter, *Music in the Universities,* opposite p. 35. The second and third from the top (bottom) are Hypate and Parhypate.

19. Oxford and Cambridge colleges supported a number of these schools, providing in their foundation charters for a certain number of boys, along with a singing-master and other musical officials: see Carpenter, *Music in the Universities, passim,* for details.

20. See Holinshed's description of Henry's musical abilities, Chapter 1, note 29, above.

21. See the *Carmen Extemporale* in Smith, *Erasmus,* pp. 453–54. And see Smith's translation of this (although the word *guitar* is an unfortunate choice), p. 62: "O Skelton, worthy of eternal fame," Erasmus begins. And he continues,

> But unto thee Apollo gave his lyre,
> Thou playest the strings taught by the Muses' choir;
> Persuasion lies like honey on thy tongue
> Given by Calliope, and thou hast sung
> A song more sweet than dying swan's by far,
> And Orpheus self yields thee his own guitar,
> And when thou strik'st it savage beasts grow mild,
> Thou leadest oaks and stayest torrents wild,
> And with thy soul-enchanting melodies
> Thou meltest rocks. . . .

22. See the excellent account of Cornish in *Grove's Dictionary of Music and Musicians* (5th ed., London, 1954). It is still uncertain whether there was one Cornish or two, but modern historians of music incline to think there was only one.

23. Hawkins prints the parable, commenting (*History of Music,* II, 508), "It seems to be a complaint of Cornish himself against one that had falsely accused him, who is distinguished by the name of Informacion, as Cornish is by that of Musike." Hawkins also comments upon the Colours of Musyke in the poem (where, oddly enough, green is in-

cluded), saying (*ibid.*, II, 509 n), "This passage should be red, blake ful, blake void, &c."

24. The recording is, unfortunately, out of print. While staying with Gerald and Patricia Coke at their beautiful home, Jenkyn Place, in Bentley, Hampshire, I had the great pleasure of hearing the music and studying the score in the splendid music library there.

25. See Chapter 1, note 17.

26. See *The Eclogues of Alexander Barclay*, ed. Beatrice White (London, 1928), pp. 165–66, for the long attack on bad poets (11. 685–718). As Miss White notes (257), "The Latin has been expanded by Barclay into what has always been considered a covert attack on his contemporary Skelton. Certainly a personal allusion of some kind is intended here, for the reference to the 'Poete laureate' is quite gratuitous."

Thomas Warton, *History of English Poetry* (London, 1774–81), II, 254, cites these lines and states that they allude to Skelton.

27. *Index*, p. 19.

28. Thomas Fuller, *History of the Worthies of England* (London, 1662), II. 257. The Latin epigram follows:

> Quid me Sceltone fronte sic aperta
> Carpis, vipereo potens veneno?
> Quid versus trutina meos iniqua
> Libras? dicere vera num licebit?
> Doctrinae, tibi dum parare famam,
> Et Doctus fieri studes Poeta,
> Doctrinam nec habes, nec es Poeta.

29. See the Huntington copy: *Here begynneth the holy lyfe and history of saynt werburge / very frutefull for all christen people to rede* (London, 1521), Cap. xxiiii. For a discussion of the meaning of inventiveness as a literary quality, see Nelson, pp. 221–22.

30. See the Huntington copy, *Here begynneth the lyfe of saynte Radegunde* (London, n.d. [1521?], fol. s. i. *verso:* "It were a pleasaunt werke for the monke of Bury / For Chaucer or Skelton / fathers of eloquens / Or for religious Barkeley to shewe theyr diligens /"

31. For a handy listing of all editions of Skelton through 1932, see Gordon, pp. 207–8. Pollet (260–62) brings the list up to 1957.

32. See Dyce, I, lxxviii–lxxix:

> Ohe, shall I leaue out Skeltons name,
>   The blossome of my frute.
> The tree wheron indeed
>   My branchis all might groe?

Nay, Skelton wore the lawrell wreath,
    And past in schoels, ye knoe;
A poet for his arte,
    Whoes iudgment suer was hie,
And had great practies of the pen,
    His works they will not lie;
His terms to taunts did lean,
    His talke was as he wraet,
Full quick of witte, right sharp of words,
    And skilful of the staet;
Of reason riep and good,
    And to the haetfull mynd,
That did disdain his doings still,
    A skornar of his kynd;
Most pleasant euery way,
    As poets ought to be,
And seldom out of princis grace,
    And great with eche degre.
Thus haue you heard at full
    What Skelton was indeed;
A further knowledge shall you haue,
    If you his bookes do reed.
I haue of meer good will
    Theas verses written heer,
To honour vertue as I ought,
    And make his fame apeer,
Than whan the garland gay
    Of lawrel leaues but laet:
Small is my pain, great is his prayes,
    And thus sutch honour gaet.

33. III, 686 and 863.

34. See fol. C. iii *verso.*

35. George Puttenham, *The Arte of English Poesie,* 1589 (Arber English Reprints, London, 1869), p. 74.

36. *Ibid.,* p. 97.

37. Francis Meres, *Palladis Tamia* (Scholars' Facsimiles and Reprints, New York, 1938), p. 279 b.

38. Henry Peacham, *The Complete Gentleman and Other Works,* ed. Virgil B. Heltzel (Ithaca, 1962), p. 107. We recall that in 1631, the antiquarian John Weever (*Ancient Funeral Monuments,* p. 476) found Skelton's epitaphs still hanging on the tombs in Westminster Abbey.

39. See especially pp. 224–25, John S. Farmer, *Six Anonymous*

Plays, First Series (London, 1905). Compare the lines of Ulysses' letter, p. 214, with the ending to the diatribe *Agaynste a Comely Coystrowne* (Dyce, I, 17): "Wryten at Croydon by Crowland in the Clay, / On Candlemas euyn, the Kalendas of May."

40. See John S. Farmer, *Six Anonymous Plays,* Second Series (London, 1906), p. 99.

41. See Michael Drayton, *Poems* (London, 1627), pp. 301–2.

42. Arber English Reprints (Westminster, 1895). See, e.g., p. 113 for heretical charges against the Cardinal, similar to Skelton's charges in *Colin Clout.*

43. Dyce, II, 400–47. For other religious poems imitating Skelton, see *ibid.,* II, 400–13, and see also E. Bischoffsberger, *Der Einfluss John Skeltons auf die englische Literatur* (Freiburg, 1914).

44. See *The Treatyse answerynge the boke of Berdes, Compyled by Collyn clowte,* ed. F. J. Furnivall, EETS (London, 1870), pp. 305–316.

45. Cf. the first footnote in E. K.'s gloss to the *Calender,* where Spenser's debt to Skelton as well as to Marot is acknowledged: "COLIN CLOVTE is a name not greatly vsed, and yet haue I sene a Poesie of M. Skeltons vnder that title. But indeed the word Colin is Frenche, and vsed of the French Poete Marot. . . ."

46. Thomas Fuller, *History of the Worthies of England* (London, 1662), I, 221.

47. See *ibid.,* I, 221 and 257–58:

> The *Dominican Friars* were the next he contested with, whose vitiousness lay pat enough for his hand; but such foul Lubbers fell heavy on all which found fault with them. These instigated *Nix* Bishop of *Norwich,* to call him to account for keeping a Concubine, which cost him (as it seems) a suspension from his benefice. . . .

Fuller relates that Skelton had children by this woman, of whom he said on his deathbed, "that in his Conscience he kept her in the notion of a wife, the such his *cowardliness* that he would rather confess *adultery,* (then accounted but a *venial;*) than own *marriage* esteemed a capital crime in that age." The reference to Lyly has already been explained: see p. 123 above.

48. Anthony à Wood, *Athenae Oxonienses, An Exact History of all the Writers and Bishops who Have Had Their Education in . . . Oxford* (London, 1691–92), I, 20–21.

49. The entire preface is well worth reading: see Gordon, pp. 200–201. It was Gordon who actually discovered this edition (only copy of which lies in the Bodleian), missed by all Skelton editors and by the Cambridge Bibliography of English Literature.

50. See pp. 48–49, beginning, "His *Bowge of Court* is, in my opinion, a Poem of great Merit: it abounds with Wit, and Imagination, and argues him well vers'd in Human Nature, and the Manners of that insinuating Place."

51. Thomas Warton, *History of English Poetry* (London, 1774–81; index, 1806), III, 336–65.

52. See her *Book of the Poets* (originally printed in the *Athenaeum,* June-August, 1842), *Poetical Works* (London, 1932), p. 633.

Selected Bibliography

Primary Sources

A complete listing of Skelton's published works, individual and collected, may be found at the end of the biographies by Nelson, Gordon, and Pollet. Only the most important works are listed below.

1. Collected Works
Pithy, pleasaunt and profitable workes of maister Skelton. London: T. Marshe, 1568. A reprint of this. London: C. Davis, 1736.
The Poetical Works. Ed. Alexander Dyce. 2 vols. London: Thomas Rodd, 1843. A reprint of this. Boston: Little Brown and Co., 1856.
The Complete Poems. Ed. Philip Henderson. London and Toronto: J. M. Dent and Sons, 1931. 2nd rev. ed., 1948; 3rd ed., 1959.
Skelton's Complete Poetical Works. Ed. Robert S. Kinsman and Edmund A. Reiss. Oxford: Clarendon Press. In preparation.

2. Selected Works (see bibliographies by Nelson, Gordon, Green, and Pollet for additional items)
A Selection from the Poetical Works. Ed. W. H. Williams. London: Isbister and Co., 1902.
Poems. Ed. Richard Hughes. London: William Heinemann, 1924.
John Skelton. Ed. Robert Graves. London: Ernest Benn, 1927. *The Augustan Books of English Poetry.* Series 2, No. 12.
John Skelton: A Selection from His Poems. Ed. V. de Sola Pinto. London: Sidgwick and Jackson, Ltd., 1950.

3. Separate Works (modern critical editions)
The Bibliotheca Historica of Diodorus Siculus, Translated by John Skelton. Ed. F. M. Salter and H. L. R. Edwards. 2 vols. EETS. London: Oxford University Press, 1956–57.
Magnyfycence. Ed. Robert Lee Ramsay. EETS. London: K. Paul, Trench, Trübner and Co., 1908.
Speculum principis. Ed. F. M. Salter. *Speculum,* IX (1934), 25–37.

Secondary Sources.

1. Biographical and Critical Works

EDWARDS, H. R. L. *Skelton: The Life and Times of an Early Tudor Poet.* London: British Book Center, 1949. This book, along with Nelson's, remains the standard biography of Skelton. It incorporates material from the author's many published articles and contains the best analysis, so far, of *Speak, Parrot.*

GORDON, IAN A. *John Skelton: Poet Laureate.* Melbourne: Melbourne University Press, 1943. A perceptive study of the man and his poetry, with little reference, however, to Skelton studies that appeared during World War II. Especially illuminating is the discussion of Philip Sparrow in relation to the Roman service books (based on material in an earlier article).

GREEN, PETER. *John Skelton.* No. 128. Writers and Their Work. London: Longmans, Green and Co., 1960. Excellent short account of the man and his poetry.

LLOYD, L. J. *John Skelton: A Sketch of His Life and Writings.* Oxford: Basil Blackwell, 1938. Brief introduction to the poet has been superseded by the works of Nelson, Edwards, Gordon, and Pollet.

NELSON, WILLIAM. *John Skelton, Laureate.* New York: Columbia University Press, 1939. Best single book on Skelton; the most satisfactory study of both poet and poetry. Here are found many of Nelson's historical discoveries and insights described earlier in separate articles.

POLLET, MAURICE. *John Skelton.* Paris: Didier, 1962. Comprehensive study incorporating much of the latest research. Especially cogent are arguments for Yorkshire as the birthplace of the poet.

2. Critical Studies (for many others not listed here, see Notes and References)

AUDEN, W. H. "John Skelton," *The Great Tudors.* Ed. K. Garvin. London: Nicholson, 1935. This excellent introduction to Skelton is to be found only in the first edition of *The Great Tudors.*

BRIE, F. "Skelton-Studien," *Englische Studien,* XXXVII (1907), 1–86. Pioneer work on Skelton, now largely out-dated.

CARPENTER, NAN C. "Skelton and Music: *Roty bully joys,*" *Review of English Studies,* n.s. VI (1955), 369–84. Discussion of Skelton as musician, based upon his citing of old chanson *Roti bouilli joyeulx* and much musical terminology in his poem "Against a Comely Coistrown."

FISH, STANLEY S. *John Skelton's Poetry.* New Haven: Yale University Press, 1965. Generally sound analysis of the poetry, with special

attention to *Speak, Parrot.* (This book was published some
months after my own MS was completed, and so I was not able to
draw upon it.)

FORSTER, E. M. "John Skelton," *Three Cheers for Democracy.* New
York: Harcourt, Brace and Co., 1951, pp. 135–53. Brilliant lecture delivered at the Aldeburgh Festival, 1950.

HARRIS, WILLIAM O. *Skelton's 'Magnyfycence' and the Cardinal Virtues Tradition.* Chapel Hill: University of North Carolina Press,
1965. (This book appeared long after my MS was completed.)

HEISERMAN, A. R. *Skelton and Satire.* Chicago: University of Chicago
Press, 1961. Solemn and detailed commentary on the major
satires.

HOLLOWAY, JOHN. "Skelton," *The Charted Mirror.* London: Routledge
and K. Paul, Ltd., 1960, pp. 3–24. The Chatterton Memorial Lecture for the British Academy. Emphasizes Skelton's break with
the aureate tradition.

KINSMAN, ROBERT S. "Phyllyp Sparowe: Titulus," *Studies in Philology,*
XLVII (1950), 473–84. Study of the relation of Skelton's poem
to the medieval mourning poem, the *titulus.*

————. "Skelton's *Magnyfycence:* The Strategy of the 'Olde
Sayde Sawe,'" *ibid.,* LXIII (1966), 99–125. Study of the use of
the proverb and *sententia* in Skelton's interlude, especially with
regard to mutability, through proverbs related to the weather and
to change.

————. "Skelton's 'Uppon a Deedmans Hed': New Light on the
Origin of the Skeltonic," *ibid.,* L (1953), 101–10. Study of the
little religious lyric as the first of the poems in Skeltonics.

————. "The 'Buck' and the 'Fox' in Skelton's 'Why Come Ye
Nat to Courte?'" *Philological Quarterly,* XXIX (1950). Political
background of the long satire: the "Buck" is Edward Stafford,
3rd Duke of Buckingham; the "Fox," Richard Fox, Bishop of Win-
chester and Lord of the Privy Seal.

————. *Skelton: The Canon and A Census of 16th Century Editions.* New York: The Renaissance Society of America. In preparation.

————. "Voices of Dissonance: Pattern in Skelton's *Colyn
Cloute,*" *Huntington Library Quarterly,* XXVI (1963), 291–313.
Finds three major voices (the poet as hero-prophet, Colyn Clout
as defender of the Church, and the tyrannical tones of Wolsey)
as anti-thesis to the thesis (sustained attack) here.

Index

DATE DUE